Mysteries of the Temple of Set

Mysteries of the Temple of Set

Don Webb

Copyright © 2004
by Don Webb

All rights reserved. No part of this book, either in part or in whole, may be reproduced, transmitted or utilized in any form or by any means electronic, photographic or mechanical, including photocopying, recording, or by any information storage and retrieval system, without the permission in writing from the Publisher, except for brief quotations embodied in literary articles and reviews.

For permissions, or for the serialization, condensation, or for adaptation write the Publisher at the address below.

Cover Design by Jamie Baglioni

Published by
LODESTAR
P.O. Box 16
Bastrop, Texas 78602

www.seekthemystery.com

Dedication

To the friends of Set in the Yet-To-Be, that they may know us and Touch our Souls in the Great Dark.

Table of Contents

Introduction	1
The Self	3
Darkness and Her Prince	6
Har-Wer	8
The Importance of Magical Practice	11
Exchange	15
Xeper	18
Other Words	22
The Degree System	30
The Future of the Aeon	36
Fourteen Notes from Neheh	39
Note One	41
Note Two	46
Note Three	48
Note Four	50
Note Five	53
Note Six	55
Note Seven	57
Note Eight	61
Note Nine	66
Note Ten	70
Note Eleven	72
Note Twelve	79
Note Thirteen	85
Note Fourteen	90
Leave Taking	94

Introduction

Unlike thousands of magical seekers in the world, I did not begin my quest by looking for groups to join. I began my quest with the direct experience of Wonder. I had seen and felt things that went beyond the ordinary. I had done things by Will alone, and encountered the Wonders done by others, which I learned to be receptive to. These matters may be dealt with elsewhere, not in this book. This book will share some of my writings in the Temple of Set during my years as High Priest. It is not a doctrinal work of the Temple.

The Temple began with a handful of people that had broke away from the Church of Satan. Almost anyone would have imagined this small group centered in California to have the average fate of any cult. It would center on a leader, immerse itself in the art of gaining as many members as possible, dumb down its teachings, and eventually factionalize again into other small groups, and have no effect on the occult world except for generating some peculiar artifacts that could be traded on e-bay.

Instead the Temple ignored the quest for members. It's founder stepped down from the High Priesthood. I was the third High Priest and I am resigning this year. We have no factions proclaiming their own doctrine, and despite the miserable misinformation that has been spread about us, we have members in 16 countries and have become one of the most influential magical lodges on the planet in the first twenty-seven years of our existence. Our teachings have grown more sophisticated. Our requirements for obtaining our internal grades have become more rigorous, our members more successful.

Yet we have maintained a great Silence about many of our teachings. It is time to lift the veil partly. There are certain moments when magical Utterances are sent into the world to change it, and you have become part of the process by simply reading this book. I'd like to talk with you about my goals for this book, some guidelines that might help you profit by it, and lastly about the book's limitations.

The book consists of two sections. The first is a general introduction to Setian theory and practice. The second are essays of mine (called Notes from Neheh) from our newsletter the *Scroll of Set*. These essays are edited to remove administrative details, and names have been removed to protect the privacy of our members. There will be future volumes in this series, which will likewise have introductory material and the essays.

I hope that this book introduces Setian thought into the world. This work is not intended as a recruitment manual for the Temple of Set, although I will provide contact information at the back of the volume. I hope that that these little books may in time have an effect on the magical world not unlike Israel Regardie's The *Golden Dawn*. My second wish would be that these books provide an introduction to Setian philosophy to those people who are uninterested in magical practice, but are sincerely interested in self-knowledge. I hope that my words may help them in their quests. If my book gives you many new questions and perhaps a few new tools, I will have succeeded. Thirdly I hope to provide information on Setian thought to students of religion. Lastly I hope that my little books may simply re-awaken Wonder in the reader. I know that Wonder has not died in you, or you would not have chanced the loss of money to buy the book, or the social outrage that having a book dedicated to the Prince of Darkness might bring you. I admire your bravery and your curiosity. With such magic as I might have I Bless you with new questions and prosperity for as long as you seek. If you feel in the end that my book has helped you I would like you to send me your blessings in return.

My book is designed for people of legal age. Not because it has any scandalous content, but because Setians believe their religion is for the changes that we can make as adults. Children have their own change processes that are best overseen by rational caring parents, who (we feel) should not over indoctrinate them in any religion. The Temple has no under age members.

If you set down and read this book cover-to-cover, you will be overwhelmed. My *Scroll* essays were released every two months, so they are very full of information. An ideal way to study this work would be to get two or three people to read it with. You can probably find the people by running an ad in your local free paper. Read an essay or two a week and then have a discussion about them. Talk about what you like, don't like, find hard or easy to understand. Most people would be too shy to try this, despite that the friendships they may gain will in themselves will more than pay for the book. This is an illustration of Setian method. You try sending your will into the Cosmos (you run the ad). You are receptive to what come to you. You engage in free-form philosophical speculation (in other words you talk about yourselves with some clergyman to interrupt it for you). You engage in discipline (you meet on a regular schedule). You deal with personal friction. All of this is a low-grade example of Initiation – and you got by acting on your own, not paying a penny to a group, not wearing a funny robe. These actions, without the trappings of mystery bring you fairly close to Mystery.

But even if you feel that you could not risk the action of gathering a discussion group, you should still read the book slowly and take breaks between the sections to think about what you have just read.

This book is not a substitute for membership in the Temple of Set. Reading these words has limits. Firstly they are the words of only one initiate. The Temple has many points of view, and those of the High Priest are not dogmatic. Secondly these words have their greatest effect in the magical and initiatory environment of the Temple of Set. There is great skiing in the Olympics and then there is reading about skiing in the Olympics.

I. The Self

The Setian views the Self as a group of forces and substances that have been unified for a season for the purpose of cultivating an immortal substance that can continue to effect both itself and the universe. Some of these substances can be identified as the body, the mind, the emotions, the social background into which a person is born, and other subtler influences that derive from magical actions of past humans. The unifying force, the force that assembled these part of you, my Gentle Reader, is the Black Flame. But "Creation" is not assembling, it is the first step to assembling. The Black Flame, the force that seeks individuality magnetized these forces and substances because they reflect some unique quality that you wanted to become manifest. Let's look at some implications of these ideas.

The reason you are here, is that part of you wants to Become. You are not a finished product. You have chosen exactly the materials you need for your becoming. God did not reward you or punish you with this life. You did not earn it through past deeds in another life. The Black Flame did not enter from an eternal perspective —you do not have foreknowledge, you do not have a destiny. This is much colder than most magical religions, which will tell you that you can not screw-up because "Fate" is running the game. However it does give you the keys to happiness and power, as you refine/express the Black Flame you continue to draw to yourself the forces and substances you need for further Becoming. In the Setian world-view the mysterious process that led to you being incarnated, is an ongoing process – and that process is manifest every time you draw something to you, whether it's working to pay for the vacation at Disneyworld or Wishing that you find a great Teacher. The process of Desire is the key to Becoming.

That key, however, only works by actions. The Self wants the easier path. It is easier to sit around and dream of what might be – and then do nothing. Imagination provides no refinement of the Black Flame, because it simply is the Black Flame. The Black Flame must be contacted, raised to a higher pitch, and then the images it produced must be sought for in the world of deeds. The process of Coming Into Being should be accompanied in most cases by something you point to, hear, weigh, smell and so forth. Setians, who are as vain as any magicians, love to brag, but they don't brag about what they might do, but rather about what they have done.

The Self must overcome obstacles in obtaining its desire. It must discover new things, both new things about the universe and the Self. Self-knowledge is the map of what goals to seek in the inner and outer worlds – and self knowledge only comes through action in the objective plain.

The substances the Black Flame chose to make its individuality out of are limited, and must be cared for. The mind, the body, family riches, the emotions – all can be drained and destroyed. The Setian must learn all the reasonable practical ways to care for these things. This in itself is a lifelong task. That means the Setian is expected to take care of the health of body, mind, emotions, and immediate environment. But there are mysterious aspects to these substances as well. The body, which is perhaps the greatest Initiator, not only teaches more about cycles and needs than a thousand books; but also is a storehouse of esoteric information. The magical will of mankind has been shaping your DNA for countless millennia. Sometimes your body will tell you if you are in the presence of a friend or an enemy. Sometimes your body will tell you that you are in a place that will be important for you. Your body will most likely pick your mate, your dwelling place and most of your friends. So it must be listened to, cared for, respected.

This is true for all of the elements that the Black Flame has chosen.

As Setians we believe that the process of Becoming can be aided by Initiation. Initiation is the process of discovering who you came into this world to be, and then Becoming that self. It is a series of processes usually begun from (apparently) outside of yourself, but then carefully chosen and designed by the self-evolving self. It can be broken down in various ways, Uncle Setnakt breaks it into four experiences, two positive and two negative. I'll give you my model, I suggest you use it until you come up with your own.

The first experience is something that catches the attention of the Black Flame, a sacred moment where the Self becomes aware of itself. This moment is usually claimed by religions of light, since they focus on the outside event, rather than the inner unfolding. Most human mysticism is based on seeking and re-experiencing this moment of illumination. Persons possessed of such moments can (by their actions) become kinder, more thoughtful, more curious about the world. Most of human goodness is a reflection of these moments, taken from the subjective experience of individuals and cast into the objective world by action. Like all positive experiences one can become addicted to his path, and then initiation ceases although as you sit for years by the side of the Ganges, the world may deem you holy.

Another positive experience comes from consciously altering the world so that others may have that same glimpse of Self, that placed on you the path of self-discovery and self-actualization. This means becoming a magician rather than a mystic, or a trickster rather than a minister. The joy that you have initiating another, is exactly like the joy the Prince of Darkness had initiating you. This is consciously using a divine prototype to bring yourself an experience that you can use for your own Becoming. The memories that you bring yourself are more lasting and permanent than the substances you choose upon entering this world. This experience too can become addictive, and you could become a cult-leader, taking your flock through illumination and illumination — and away from the world of action in the real world.

The negative experience of self-knowledge is discovering how messed-up you are. Humans are vastly imperfect creatures. We have developed great defenses against seeing our flaws. As the Magus Jesus said we overlook the beams in our eyes while focusing on the sawdust in another's. He was right in that the flaws of others that madden us the most, are our own flaws – rubbing up our defense mechanisms. The real Initiate is always on the lookout for methods to sneak past his or her defenses and see what is really wrong. The negative vision of the building blocks of the Self, is terrifying and harsh. It can lead to depression and anger, yet the Initiate learns to take as calmly as he or she can and begin to work on strategies to short-circuit the behaviors that stand in the way of his or her desire. The danger with the negative vision is that we are willing to substitute suffering for work. "I don't know how to change myself so I'll do penance." People who encounter the negative vision often seek to punish themselves. Initiates seek the negative vision in order to find out what to work on. (Like the positive vision of the self, the negative vision usually comes form outside first – a bad report card, a crappy job, a car wrapped around a telephone pole, etc.)

The fourth part of Initiation is choosing a negative aspect of the world to struggle against. Early in out Initiation we have two sorts of bad things to struggle against. We have to struggle to make our way in the world – get a house, an education, money for the baby-sitter, etc. Desire provides simple crude and plentiful energy for these struggle. We also have to struggle against things in our characters that are weak and hurtful. We have to overcome the legacy of an abusive parent, or end our relationship with drugs, or simply learn how not to be lazy. Desire provides less energy for that, because these flaws usually come about because we misrouted energy in the first place. But the energy that we produce to overcome these problems is much more useful to the Self in its quest for immortality. But the Self needs more. The Self needs to feel that it can make big changes. So the Initiate looks around his or her world. What problem strikes deeply at the Self? What problem does his or her Black Flame rebel against? It could be the environment, or the state of women in the world, or religious intolerance, or any of a thousand things. Pick that worst problem and apply yourself against it. Not as a simple drudge, but as a general with a plan. Maybe your first year begins by picking up Styrofoam cups on Earth Day, but your tenth year might be making a video about deforestation. This sort of work is far too hard for the occultnik, that would rather wave his wand bless the redwoods and go home. I have called this experience a "negative" one because despite the positive victories and celebrations along the way, you will always having the humbling truth that the world can not be fixed, no matter how powerful you become in it. Desire provides almost no energy for these tasks, you have to provide Desire by magic. You have to learn how to create your own energy not based on body needs or social inventory. But if you learn to produce and use such energy while alive — you will have the skill you need after death to produce desire, channel desire, accept and learn from your deeds and proceed to victory. That is the process of Initiation.

The Temple provides a meaningful context for this process to take place. It provides the first two experiences as part of its magical training. The great mystical moment can be passed from Mouth to Ear at any Setian Working, particularly the great annual Working at Conclave. These illuminations most often do not happen in the chamber, but as a result of the energies unleashed into the world by these workings. Of course the world benefits by our Working, but lacking the knowledge of what to look for, they miss those moments when they appear. The Temple provides a context for the second sort of positive experience by letting Setians of all degrees write rituals for their personally determined Needs. It provides a specific place for the second sort of positive experience by having an institutionally created Priesthood. It provides a social network that helps people avoid undo fascinations with any of the four experiences of Initiation, and beyond this it provides a magical framework where in great synchronicities occur for Setians. It creates omens, coincidences, and opportunities that show up "magically' while people are doing their Self work. All of this occurs in the magical environment that is connected with the Prince of Darkness.

II. Darkness and Her Prince

The Temple is dedicated to the Prince of Darkness. Mankind gained its awareness from the Prince as a Gift, and has been so shocked at the Gift that the Prince has been relegated into various bogyman roles like Satan and Tchort. Some cultures have seen It more positively as Set, Tezcatlipoca or Kali. But the Mystery of this figure goes beyond any label or cultural fad.

It is not a guy in red tights that tempts you to do bad things.

It is the God of imagination.

Picture a vast expanse of darkness – space without light. Within is a great intelligence that knows only one thing. It has Come Into Being. It can perceive itself, and it has only one faculty, imagination. It can fancy itself to be this or that, and it can dream of what is yet-to-be. This being had certain choices. It could become one with the darkness around it – spreading its consciousness so thin as to be nothing. It could choose to be alone for all of time, or it could choose to create others. It chose the later. Its method was not science but magic. It had discovered that imagination can become reality. Or to use current Setian terms, "A change in the subjective universe can produce a proportionate change in the objective universe." The Prince of Darkness's first creation was the Prince of Light. We will discuss this force later.

The Prince of Darkness's second creation was sentient life in the realm of the Prince of Light. This life came into being by giving certain life-forms an imperishable sense of individuality. This Gift is one of imagination. In the realm without imagination there is no immortality. In the realm without imagination there is no desire. Imagination brings about desire, because it suggest the possibility of other things. In the realm of no imagination there is no art, no music, no strife, no envy, no delight in puzzling about darkness. All the things that make us good and bad as human beings, all the things that set us up for a life beyond the realm of light, all the things that allow us to do things beyond the ordinary rules of the world come from the Gift of the Prince of Darkness.

We can know the Prince in three ways. The first manner is self-knowledge. As we explore the workings of our spirit, we are exploring the shape of the Prince of Darkness. As we expand our imagination we encounter all the things It encountered. We encounter loneliness. We encounter the desire to know things, and the mix of frustration/delight when we discover the more we know the more there is to know. We discover the mystery of magic – that those things we imagine come about in mysterious ways. We discover that we become fascinated with the world, yet belong to it less and less because we become more abstract and eternal. We discover that we have to be True to ourselves. Because the standards of our selves are ultimately what shapes the world around us. Like the Prince of Darkness we must shape the world in accordance with who we truly are. Most people who try to shape the world in accordance with models other than their own, become more and more unhappy. They sicken and die, having lived only (as did their ancestors' ancestors) to produce offspring. This nature of the Will has been clear to mankind at various times. The Magus Nietzsche gave us a fairly good picture. The Magus Crowley tried to set the world free by making it clear with: Do What Thou Wilt Shall Be The Whole Of The Law. But he did not understand that the universe is likewise coming to reflect the Prince of Darkness more clearly, just as the circumstances of our lives come to reflect ourselves. Fortunately our Will, a product of the Gift is in harmony with the Gift at the best and highest levels of our selves. We can through self-knowledge, come to understand the purpose of the Prince of Darkness and align our goals with It to achieve a great cosmic boost. Learning to do this is the goal of Setian religion. By being Awake to our own shaping of the universe and making conscious choices to align our choices with those of Set, we further Its goals and our own. We don't loose our individuality in the process, but rather enhance it by adding more power to our own chosen endeavors. I choose to expand Magus Crowely's Law thusly: Do What Thou Wilt Shall Be The Whole Of The Law. Great Is The Might Of Set, Greater Still He Through Us.

A second way to know the Prince of Darkness is through history. There are moments in human history when change rapidly flows through the world that expands personal freedom, power and knowledge. The events of ancient Greece from the time of the great playwrights to Aristotle show the hand of the Prince of Darkness, as does the founding of the United States, the Medici Academy, or the transition form bronze to iron. We can see certain factors present in such times: the secrete society, the openness to exotic ideas, the interest in the imagination, the commitment to take the products of the mind into the objective world by action. We can see how the Prince of Darkness works, and we can therefore learn two things. We can learn what the Prince of Darkness is like, and we can learn his techniques for changing our world. For example the given items can be used by anyone wanting to change their corporate culture, their city or their university. (One of the irritating things about the Temple of Set to most occultniks is that we encourage serious university-level study of history and anthropology.

The third, and most dangerous method, by which the Prince of Darkness can be known is by simply talking to It. The Setian is not in the habit of having constant chats with the Prince of Darkness – anymore than you would causally call up the President. Such moments of exchange are very rare, For most people only once or twice in a lifetime. This is the time when certain information can be gained for self-and world change that is truly beyond you. The method is distressingly simple. It does not require ceremony or trappings. It requires Need. Setians must have a Need that they can not achieve on their own. The Need must be of an abstract nature – in other words Set doesn't chat with you about investment tips, health issues, or give you relationship advice. Set can give you information about the Cosmos, if you have a need for the information. You need only ask. But be forewarned. Such information does not come in shapes that you can easily show to another person. It may come only as feelings and hunches, found scrolls, or well timed signals from the outer world. It is very difficult to be Awake to hear such signals, and harder still not to filter the signal through your own concerns. Most people can only receive a few simple ideas such as they truly exist, the Prince of Darkness exists, personal immortality is real and so forth. As words on the page these ideas look small and simple. As real knowledge – known as a fact to the Self – they are great sources of energy and can enable to change the world and more importantly the self.

III. Har-Wer

The Prince of Light, whom Setians call Har-Wer after the ancient Egyptian god Horus the Elder, is a strange and fitful being. It is the commonality of mankind. All of us are like one another. We have the same problems, the same humanity. Many of the fragile egos that pursue the occult would deny this. Surely their problems are worse than anyone else's. The Prince of Light is seen as the author of that which is not individual. It is the structure of our brains, the programming aspects of our languages and our non-verbal communications. It is the source of ideas that sweep through crowds. It is both our ally and enemy.

One of the magical aspects of Har-Wer is the ability of mankind to create group spirits. These are usually in the business of oppressing mankind's individuality. If you have ever had the opportunity to watch a mob, you have seen Har-Wer. Har-Wer is the spirit behind corporations, nationalism, racism – pretty much any "ism." These groups have a raw magical power that makes them cohere. There is a real force that makes mankind act as a herd animal. This force is the easiest thing for a human being to invoke. You (like me) probably invoke it every night when you flip on your TV set. Others invoke it by going to a football game, or church or Las Vegas. The force makes humans always want a group. It makes them huddle together at night. It makes them stupid and afraid to try new things.

It has also, and without a doubt, made the race of man survive.

For most people their religious nature if caught up in idolizing this force. They see it in kindness and thoughtfulness for others. They wish when they die that they are reabsorbed into the force of light, or at least achieve a divine hypostatis with that force. What they don't understand is that same force produces moroseness, low self-esteem, timidity and fear. Har-Wer has given us Its mind, and we are bound by it. Any attempt to work magic with this force leads not to wakefulness, but to more exotic forms of sleep. Since most occultists worship the Prince of Light, they engage in Sleep, and their "work" is rightly despised by groups seeking wakefulness.

The religious aspect of this force teaches methods of self-annihilation. These religions are referred to as the Right Hand Path.

One might assume that Setians despise Har-Wer. Nothing could be further from the truth. Har-Wer's positive forces are needed by the Setian for their advancement, and struggling against Har-Wer's negative forces is what makes Setians strong. Let's look at each of these things. But first Uncle Setnakt hears some of your grumbling, "None of this is new I saw it in *The Matrix*", or (if you want to impress me) "This is Plato's Cave metaphor." You are correct. I am not telling you something new. I can also tell you that there will be others who will tell you the same thing long after my body is dust used to patch a knothole.

The positive aspects of Har-Wer are the secret of timing, the secret of a group, the pre-made magical matrix, and the self-sustaining working. In the world of light, the law of three prevails. The trinity of chaos is Birth-Life-Death. Everything that you see today will be gone. (This simple fact is the heart of Buddhism). The Setian can take heart in knowing that bad situations will pass away, but she can take greater heart in knowing that she can plant her Will in the world at the right time to be assured of harvest. This is great news – as humans we are capable of very small feats, but if we know when to use our precious moments of self-mastery then we can get a very full yield. This is the secret of timing. Massive groups of humans are swept along by forces they don't understand – war, depressions, booms, movements for civil rights, movements of oppressive sexism. The power of these movements is much greater than the power of the man or woman at the helm. Any group has a spirit, that arises out of the group – and generally seeks to achieve goals other than the stated goals of the group. However Setians, because they have studied the history of dozens of occult movements, are aware that consciousness can be added to these egregores. The Temple, as well as its sub-units Pylons, Orders and Elements, have group spirits that work the world just like any other group. They do our recruiting for us. One of them may be tapping you on the shoulder right now. This is the secret of a group. Har-Wer manifests in secret connections between things. If you meet someone that you like, just because you liked the last person you met with that name, you are experiencing the manifestation of Har-Wer. Har-Wer connects all of mankind together, and that means that all the magical work of mankind is still "out-there"— a vast band of connections that you can use. When you pick up the Runes or the *I-Ching* or spells from the magical papyri you are connected to the other users. Their magical world can be explored by you. There is vast power for the beginner. This is the pre-made magical matrix. Har-Wer tends toward stasis. In this tendency he is properly called Osiris, whom many neo-pagan groups worship. Stasis is not something the Setian desires for himself, but stasis can be very useful if it is put in your service. If you can construct your plans so that forces in the world can be attracted to carry it on, stasis is your ally. The freedom-loving progressive United States is an example of a self-sustaining Working. It may not always work at the high level that Franklin and Jefferson imagined it, but it keeps on going and (despite the efforts of many of our politicians) continues to attract hard working idealists from time to time.

The negative aspects of Har-Wer that provide friction to work against are hypnosis, state dependent memory, false dialogue, large scale disturbance, and delusions of power and freedom. Hypnosis is the power to create a trance. All human beings enter trance very easily. In fact of we could not enter such states, simple tasks like driving would be impossible. Unfortunately we can also enter into trance when choosing our mate, choosing our employer or having a deeply important discussion with our parents. The Setian realizes the source of hypnosis is having repetitive thoughts and actions, and in order or bring more consciousness to her life fights against hypnosis by trying new things, travel, education and methods suggested by Crowley and Gurdjieff. Each act of Will to stay awake not only increases the joy of being here, but also trains the psyche how not to fall into a rut in the next world. State dependent memory is a great curse on mankind. Most psychotherapies deal with this problem. Simply put people react to a new situation dependent on how they acted the last time they felt the same way. If you fell in love during springtime and flowers – you will feel love during springtime and flowers – quite possibly for the wrong person. If your dad made you stand out in the rain the day you wrecked his car, you may suddenly fly into a rage at your kid when you are caught outside in a rainstorm. Setians learn to fight state dependent memory by learning to self-inventory. Why do I *really* feel this way? Am I really mad at the person in front of me or at the guy that stole my bicycle when I had had too many snow-cones? Learning to fight state dependent memory (or to invoke the memory you want) is another step to being free from the world in order to act in it. False dialogue is the method whereby we enslave each other. It consists of exchanges and phrases that have been repeated so often that they have no meaning. It is coupled with paying attention only to one's internal state while trying to connect to the feelings of another. False dialogue kills love, one of the treasures of this world and a worthy goal of Black Magic. Large scale disturbances like war, plague, depression are too massive for any one magician (or even a small group of magicians) to turn away. Magicians come to the feeling early in their careers that they can do anything (see delusions of power and freedom below) so when an economic downturn takes their job away they think they can just wish it back. They don't appreciate that the movements of Har-Wer are tides, which they can either surf or be drowned by. The Setian with a keen sense of history knows that she will face three or four large scale disturbances in her life. She practices getting along in any situation, firstly by imagination and then by acquiring some practical skills. This means that when bad times roll across the land, they don't steamroll over the Setian. Delusions of power and freedom are the chief means that Har-Wer stops individual accomplishment. It causes people to think that they have a great deal of control over their lives. Some will even tell you that they are a "god." These delusions cause people to be sloppy, lazy and stupid. As soon as they have the least bit of attainment they slack off the magical path. Such people are often "at war" with other magicians that they feel have slighted them in some way. Of course in this as in all of Har-Wer's tricks we all have it. Setians (at their best) merely know that they will fall for it sometimes, and hope that no sees them do so.

Har-Wer gives us great power and great challenges.

IV. The Importance of Magical Practice

The Temple of Set has all things that could make a very popular new religion. It emphasizes self-improvement, it has a cool gothic aesthetic, it has brainy initiates, and it's "naughty" enough to be interesting – while still having a strong ethical base, so you can tell your boss, mom, or college adviser that you are a member. But it has one thing that keeps it from moving up the charts – it not only believes in the existence of, but tests its members ability in the practice of magic. Now magic is very unpopular. This is true for three reasons. Since Late Antiquity the state and church have had a vested interest in discoursing magical practice. For one thing magic works very well to create attitudes, from a pep rally to Mass, magic can unify human endeavor. So you don't want that technology in just anyone's hands. Secondly as was well known in Late Antiquity, magic simply works. It doesn't work as well as the TV versions, and frankly can't beat technology in most objective world changes, but it does work – and you definitely don't want a power source not built on wealth and position floating around in the world. So magic was suppressed, magical books and magicians burned, and magical practice driven underground. If you need to test how well the Roman Empire is still up and working, just tell a group of people at a layover bar in an airport that you practice magic, and watch them all move away from your stool.

The second reason that magic is unpopular is that it requires talent. While many, perhaps most human beings, can when pressed perform a magical act – only those with an extra dose of the Black Flame can reliably perform magic. Sadly the easiest way to get that extra dose is to have a lonely childhood, which caused you to use the heck out of your imagination. So magicians trend to be outcasts with some socialization problems – not exactly the group that will overturn the cultural attitudes above, but we're working on it. Since many people may try their hand at magic and fail, it becomes important for them to speak against it. If they have the urge, but not the talent, they are happier in a large group that does low wattage group ceremonies. That way they can feel moved, and not have to deal with their lacks.

The third reason that magic is unpopular is that is dangerous. Nothing you will do can stir up your soul like magic. Talented magicians can spin out in a couple of ways, if they are practicing magic without mentoring and a community that understands magic. The first way, the Sorcerer's Apprentice Syndrome, comes from liberally applying magic to objective situations. You cast a spell to make Shelly fall in love with you. She does so and you find out that she is obsessive, jealous and stupid. So you cast a spell to get out of your life, and you are transferred to Moosejaw, Alaska in December, so you cast a spell for a better job . . . and so in widening spirals of disaster. The second type of spinout is the Super-Therapist approach. Persons wanting to work on themselves cast all of their energy inward to quickly fix some personal problems that took decades to develop. They cast a spell that takes all of their defects and burns them away – without figuring out what those defects defended their psyches against, and what better moods and emotions could be used to in their place. This would be the psychic equivalent of throwing away a ratty old coat in the middle of the coldest night of the year, and then freezing to death.

Now that we have seen the objections to magic, why practice it?

It can make your life better.

It can make you aware of who you really are.

It can help you change some things about yourself, and correctly manifest other things.

It can convince you that you belong to an order of life that is greater than what you see around you, and have been taught to perceive by the forces of Har-Wer.

The first point is pretty easy. Yes, magic can help you get that job, boyfriend, or heal your gout. Now it won't help a 52 year old start his pro football career, or a grow you a new leg. It is subject to the laws of the objective universe, when cast into the objective universe. It impartially and neutrally (or as the popular saying goes, "Be careful what you wish for you might just get it!").

The second point is tougher to grasp. Unless you are committed to the Setian goal of personal immortality, the use of magic to discover who you are seems a little odd. Lets look at something in the objective world. If you are buying a computer, you need to know its price, its capabilities, the space it will take up on your desk, what software comes with it, what guarantees, what experiences others have had with it. If you can get enough of these facts you can make an informed purchase and you will use the system better. You need the facts about your soul much more desperately if you are going to experience eternity in it. Your questions may be simple, but not knowing them is painful. "What spiritual qualities do I have because I'm Irish? Why don't I like girls? Am I more afraid of being alone when I die or being married to someone I hate? How can I be nicer to my spouse? How can I remember my dreams? What do I really want?" All of these things can be found through magic, if you can learn to receive signals from the universe as well as send them. Setians are encouraged to do the first sort of magic first. This gives them a reason to trust what the Temple is telling them, and to learn about how magic works before they turn it on themselves.

The third reason, learning how to change yourself, is tougher still. People can only Become what they Are. Like an acorn that will only grow into an oak, people have definite characteristics that are hidden in the spark of individuality we call the Black Flame, but they have many characteristics that have been forced upon them. They may have been taught they are stupid or unhappy or lazy. They may have been told that they can't learn to paint, or are bad at games, or can't learn languages. Magic is great in overcoming bad programming. Likewise they may have Hidden talents and wants, that they haven't discovered. Magic is very good for remanifesting what has been hidden.

The last point — that you can use magic to realize that you belong to an order of life, that is greater than the world of three dimensions and five senses — is crucial to Setian thinking. Setians take *a priori* that humans are not part of the natural order. Humans, because of their capacity to respond to the world in non-mechanistic ways, are viewed as unnatural. This is why we revere the Prince of Darkness, a rebel against cosmic law, as our Patron. Most people can intellectually grasp the idea that humans transcend the natural world, but magic allows them to experience it. The wholeness of being that is needed to cast one's will into the worlds, and the receptivity to see one's will return are states that have to rise beyond the natural experience. Only by experience this divine state, can one engage in the Left Hand Path practice of self-deification.

Let's try a little magic. You and I.

Turn off the TV, cell phone, anything that beeps or buzzes.

Light four candles. A red one for the life force, a black one for the black flame, a white one for the purity of your purpose, and a gold one for the human world in all its complexity.

Say nothing till your mind is calm, and you can think of nothing for reasonable periods.

Then say in a pleasing clear voice, "I seek after the mysteries of my own becoming. I seek after the secrets of perfection inside me, and hidden from me throughout the universe. I call to all parts of myself to make a four-fold wish."

"I wish that as I read this book, that I will become luckier. I wish that I will learn something about myself that I have not known. I wish that I will learn a magical technique I have not known. I wish that Setnakt's books sell well."

"My four-fold wish was effecting mankind before the first flint was knapped. My four-fold wish was effecting the most distant lands of the earth even know. My four-fold wish echoes into the future blessing all who wish I have wished. My four-fold wish has changed my black heart. I have never seen the day that I did not get my wish."

Then pick up each of the candles and blow them out, visualizing your wish as traveling in the given direction.

>Gold: West.
>Red: South.
>White: East.
>Black: North

This little ritual has already taught yourself a great deal. Some of you were afraid to try it. Others thought it was too silly. Others simply spoke the words aloud, too lazy to buy four candles. Others live in life circumstances that they can't even have ten minutes of control of their environment. Others tried it without believing that it will work, and will be confused that it works without belief despite what they may think about magic. Others still refused to say anything about my books because they don't believe that a single erg of energy should be used to help anyone else. Others are looking forward to the luck, others still doubt that there is anything to this except psychology. Some people felt something, others felt nothing. Others want to teach their friends to do the ritual, and it will be tried either seriously or as a party piece.

That's a lot of self knowledge from a very few words. For people who did the ritual there will be questions. Can I be sure that I'm luckier – did the ritual make me when $5.00 at scratch-off? Did I really learn something because of the ritual, or is it inevitable that reading a book about a different belief system than my own, I would learn something. Is Setnakt just programming me to tell people to buy his books?

You have entered a liminal state. You have broken away from the madding crowd, entered a world where things worked differently, and now you are awaiting the results of your ritual to re-integrate you into the world. Now you have your intellect, your imagination, and your will power to transform yourself. If you can find these feelings in yourself, you can understand why magical practice is important to the Setian.

V. Exchange

Set is the god of isolate intelligence.

The pain of the Cosmos comes from knowing on the deepest levels that we stem from a greater power, but are not ourselves as great/joyous/smart, etc. as that power. In the religions of the Right Path it is held that we can return to that power either by divine hypostasis (as in Christianity) or loss of the illusion of separation (as in Hinduism). However the followers of the Left Hand Path assume that we are sent forth not as food for our creator, but to refine intelligence.

The Cosmos is vast, mainly unknown, and most importantly subject to the powers of creation. We can make things and ideas and share them with those of our kind. We can enjoy the creations of others, without falling into the animal traps of jealousy or denial. We make the universe more strange and beautiful.

Part of the Gift of Set is the command to enjoy life, to create to explore and to share these things with people most capable of the fullest enjoyment thereof. Hence the Temple does attract artists and musicians, philosophers and writers – but it attracts anyone with a certain hunger – as long as they are not mere consumers.

The majority of out-pouring of the creative soul will of course be aimed at the greater universe. The artists will seek her gallary shows, the writer and scientist publication, the chef his own restaurant and so forth. The Temple is not an "achievement club" where one's being is measured by these sendings into the Objective Universe, rather they are understood to be the logical and necessary by-product of one's development.

Likewise it is assumed that one seeks better products for the self. The soul needs nourishment, and the evolving soul seeks better things for itself. The Setian manifests this in pursuing education in the arts and sciences. This has given the Temple a frankly "geeky" reputation among occultists. Unlike the typical occultist who waits breathlessly for the next mass-produced occult book, the Setian tends to pursue quests. The runic-minded Setian visits Uppsala, the Egyptophile goes to Set's Temple in Ombos, Egypt: the astronomer builds her own observatory, the country music fan arranges concerts.

In this notion of greater outpourings and greater feast-taking, is a map to life development. The Setian understands that she must place herself in arenas where the greatest things are possible. She may begin her career here as an 18 year old burger flipper without a GED, in a bad relationship with a man whose idea of foreplay is buying her two 40s rather than one – but she has to long for a better life and know that she needs to end her openness to such soul-degrading things as soon as possible. From the first step of herself summoning the idea/example that a better future is possible, she may wind up in a arty school. She will have traded the bad ideas that held her for better ideas hidden within her.

However this widening spiral through the objective universe is not enough.

There are two things that are needed to complete understanding of exchange. Firstly one needs to know about true and false receptivity and secondly about the need for a meso-cosmos. Let's look at each of these.

A great symbol for the conscious mind is fire. In the Temple we symbolize this by the Black Flame, the Gift of Set. But since you are not in the Temple, lets use the *I-Ching* ideogram:

$$\equiv\!\equiv$$

There are two *yang*-lines on the outer edges. This is the conscious mind sending out its products into the objective universe. But there is a *yin* line in the middle. This is **false** receptivity. When our conscious minds come into being on earth, we have an installation of social values and receptivity necessary to learning. We trust our teachers, our family, our ministers, our policemen. Could you imagine how long it would have taken you to learn the alphabet if you were allowed to ask "Why does this letter follow that letter?"— twenty five times? This part of our consciousness was socially constructed to be receptive to authority figures. It is "faith." The initiate must unlearn to avoid un-thinking responses to the world. They don't believe 100% of the evening news, the Bible, the newspaper, or the prejudices of their family. The path to end these unwanted exchanges is antinomianism – forced breaking with society, by adopting the symbols and trappings of Satan. All human beings have a moment in their lives when they try to become conscious, it is usually when they go through puberty, and such offensive symbols become dear to them. However they don't need much fire to bake them into the people they need to be, and such rebellion ends. The need for rebellion ends, and they have as much consciousness at their disposal as they are going to get. (This is why most people stop having free thought after college). The Setian needs a firmer break, which has two negative consequences. The first is that the outer door of our religion will always look adolescent, and they we will offend those people whose self-importance is too high to become their real Selves. The second trap is that such symbols are only aids, and people can spin out into seeing them as the reality they refer to, rather than mere symbols. Such people tend to leave the Temple and found their own satanic cults which have been historically short lived.

However just as society installs false receptivity, it also installs false resistance. The Temple symbolizes receptivity with the Graal. However since you are not of the Temple let's consider the *I-Ching* ideogram for water:

Two *yin*-lines guard the edges. Water is receptive since all things flow into it, and it seeks itself. However there is a *yang*-line in the center blocking reception. This is the socially constructed line that needs reception to the spiritual and magical. There is a taboo in our society against observing certain things. Talking about your dream-life or your spirituality to you co-workers is forbidden. Looking into certain magical matters is highly forbidden. This block is placed in human consciousness to limit the number of true wizards and priests, so that our society is not too chaotic. The initiate must learn to remove this block to be open to his spiritual impulses and to the magical phenomena both inside of himself and outside of himself. Receptivity is hard, because it requires real work to put yourself in the right place at the right time to receive.

These elements must by combined correctly. Here is the **wrong** form:

Here we see the average occultist. He has divorced his reasoning conscious mind form his mystic heart. So he feels impelled to act on random hunches and impulses that come from beneath his consciousness, but remain unseen to him. He thinks that he is in control, but in reality the magical impulses of the universe are in control.

Here is the desired configuration:

Consciousness is at the base of everything. No action happens save from the base, and it looks upward into the magical things it has attracted to itself. It is not moved by the magic of others, but is a free agent seeing their magic and deciding whether to act in accordance with it. The Graal is sought-for, not the hidden basis of magic. (Followers of the Northern Mysteries may wish to compare this image to that of Odhinn's eye in the base of Mimir's Well.)

Now that we've touched on the basis of true receptivity, we need to look at the meso-cosmos. Many, many would-be occultists never grasp this. If a person wants to benefit through exchange, they both need an audience and mentors. Now some mentors are available through books or other recorded media, but your time with them is limited. You don't get a chance to see them face-to-face, work out your training with them, check out if they are indeed enlightened souls and so forth. In short you have to empower such teachers by imagining them to be great people. (You are like the badly-configured hexagram). But if you choose to be part of a school you can see these people first hand. You can see more than the leader, read more than her books. It is both exhilarating and disappointing, because our heroes close-up are never as fine looking as the imaginary figures we create for ourselves. It is difficult to learn from real humans, and most humans have nowhere the guts for it.

Likewise the Initiate possesses a need for a good audience. You can talk about your aspirations and troubles to the world at large – you can even set up a website and pour your troubles out to the set that lives on cola and chips and surfs for hours. But the soul actually needs real appreciation (or as we say in the Temple: Recognition). For some things you have to have an audience of your peers. For this you need a society of magicians if you would be a magician.

So for certain exchanges the school must exist. The Temple is not a luxury for its members, it is a necessity.

Note: For students of the *I-Ching:* for the Initiate Fire (Li – Clinging) becomes Heaven (Ch-in – Creative), and Water (Keeping Still – K'an) becomes Receptive (Earth – K'un). The correct form of Earth over Heaven is Tai (Peace), the eleventh hexagram. In the west this is symbolized by the inverted or Pythagoras Pentagram: ⛥ The incorrect form Heaven over Earth is Bi (Standstill), the twelfth hexagram symbolized in the West by the upright pentagram ☆ .

VI. Xeper

The eternal and self-renewing word of Set is Xeper. It is pronounced "Kheffer."

It has existed at various times in the historical past, and was Heard and re-Uttered in 1975 by Michael A. Aquino/ Ra-En-Set and in 1997 by Don Webb/Setnakt.

We'll look at the word and its effect, and then at its form in modern times.

In the Egyptian language it means "I have come into being." It is the verb form of the noun *Khefra*, which was the beetle shaped god of dawn. He was said to be self-created, each morning. He is the epitome of all the feelings dawn invokes – new day, opportunities, hope, having made through the terrors of the night, etc. His animal, the dung beetle, gathers shit to lay its eggs in. Pushing its little dung ball, it must be like the sky god, pushing the sun across the heavens. The earliest tombs of the Egyptians were built like the dung beetles hole so that the pharaoh would rise up like the beetle. He was the earliest symbol of a powerful life after death. The Egyptian scarab is the most commonly found amulet among the dead, symbolizing their hope for rebirth.

The word contains two ideas, which are the key both to Setian practice and understanding of the Cosmos. The words are Being and Becoming.

Being is a state like the new sun. It illumines everything, including itself. Being is a state of consciousness that is both self-reflecting – its own source of illumination, as well as the means by which the universe is perceived. In moments of Being, persons know who they are on all levels from the most mundane to the most cosmic. They understand their relationship with the universe, and they are indifferent to the universe and filled with bliss at themselves. Their self-love shines forth and perceptions are vast and accurate. Being is the goal of the Setian. The state of Being is idealistic rather than realistic, or in Setian terminology Subjective rather than Objective. However unlike most idealistic systems the reality of the universe is accepted. Matter cannot sully the absolute, nor is it unreal. However matter is seen as less durable than Being. Setians believe that Being is inherent in all sentient Beings, however the fetters of the world keep this state from being enjoyed. There is that in every human that transcends the gods, yet is kept from mankind by mankind's laziness, ignorance and fear of the unknown.

Becoming is the active state whereby more Being may be obtained. Based on the inherent patterns of self, that one discovers by the light of Being, the Setian seeks to Be more. The job of the psyche is to expand and refine itself. This is not done by contemplation of Being but by expressing Being in the objective realm. The commerce of daily life is not shunned not despised but seen as the means to growth. Desire is not seen as something to be transcended, as in Buddhism, but a necessary and energizing force. However it is not a simple animal desire. It is not desire "for" something – it is desire "to" something. All desires that lead to expansion of the self are seen as good – not only love and compassion but also jealousy and anger. Becoming is the dark side of Setian practice because it may mean conflict, and hearkens back to Set's function as a god of storm and war.

These two pulses of light and dark, of Being and Becoming, are the forces by which Set brought consciousness into being, and by which the universe is expanded. They are the troubling spirit in mankind – both bringing forth beautiful cathedrals and awesome pyramids as man seeks to contemplate his Being through the products of his imagination, which he calls gods and leading to wars and atrocities where man seeks to increase his being (often by ignorant means). For the most part forces exist in balance with the natural aspects of mankind. When there is balance there is no knowledge of Set, and his name is forgotten, and Xeper is not a goal.

However that balance was lost to the universe in our times.

In 1966, Howard Levey, under his magical name of Anton Szandor LaVey began experimenting with formulas of belief and desire, the forbidden and the unknown and founded the Church of Satan. He re-Uttered Ayn Rand's word of Indulgence, which we will examine in the next essay. As part of the eternal nine year cycle of Becoming and Being, he unleashed a new period of Becoming: based on desire. With little management or expertise on his part, his Working grew into a respectable little movement. His word stressed the importance of desire, and he saw it as a key to his own wealth. Wealth, however seldom comes to magicians because of their magic alone, and he sought to supplement his income by selling offices in the Church of Satan. This fundamentally challenged the heart of (what was to Become) Setian teachings – it represented elevating desire "for" over desire "to." Levey's lieutenant was Magister Caverni Michael Angelo Aquino, who realized that the Church of Satan was not meant to be a personal expression (an instrument of Becoming), but something that had its own reason-to-exist in the objective realm (an instrument of Being). Aquino tried arguing with the boss, but to no avail, so he sought help elsewhere.

Setians do not knock on Set's door very often. Such knocking comes with a price, because it heralds a new cycle of Becoming, and an end to the bliss of self-contemplation. Set's reflection to Aquino was a document called the *Book of Coming Forth by Night*, containing the law of his Aeon *Xepra Xeper Xeperu*. It was a phrase from the *Book of Felling Apep* inscribed on the back of a statue of the Pharaoh Ramses III, son of the Pharaoh Setnakt. The verbal structure is difficult to render into English, but it contains the relationship of Being and Becoming, and the means by which the Being and Becoming of one consciousness will populate the Cosmos with other thinking/ free-willed beings. The phrase may be translated as, "I, the self-created, have come into being and my remainfestations have come into being each as self-created, by my coming into being." Aquino's blissful period of Being was at an end, and Set has chosen him as His Magus to found the Temple of Set and proclaim the word that explained the Cycle of Becoming that began ten years before in 1966 C.E. (or I Ae.S)

The shape of the word is significant. In 1966, a reprinting of E. Wallis Budge's *Easy Lessons in the Egyptian Language* contained the phrase. Budge had included as an example of stative verbs in Egyptian as well as an example of how much information could be contained in a fairly short phrase. LaVey had suggested that good ritual material could be found in books on mythology and Aquino had bought the book to spice up his group rituals. Aquino had noted the phrase, which resonated with his background in existentialism and his forays into Plato. What he did not know, since Budge hadn't labeled his sources was that the phrase was from a spell designed to vanquish Sets' foe Apep, and that French scholars had determined that Hermetic tradition of "as above, so below" came from this phrase.

Aquino did not know who Apep was either. In late Egypt Apep was a synonym of Set – a bad guy to be avoided. But in archaic Egypt Apep was the god of what did not exist. For the Setian everything exists internally. Even a fantasy has existence because it exists inside of the subjective universe. Apep originally appeared to the most ancient Egyptians as a great serpent that kept one's eternal soul from climbing a mountain and leaping off into the realm of Glowing lights. The way to stop this being from tearing you apart was to assert your own existence, your own participation in the pulse of Being/Becoming. The theory of Setian magical practice is held in this phrase as well as the Setian's mandate for action. For the Setian magic is an intense apprehension of Being, a deep and profound ecstasy, which may be aided by ritual or setting, this intense self-seeing changes the inner universe. The fundamental change there will cause a change in the objective realm. The mechanism of that change requires action on the Setian's part – each moment of blissful Being heralds a new cycle of Becoming.

Budge, an interesting character in his own right, had been a member of the Golden Dawn, and had intended his popular books on Egyptology to inspire magicians and artists as well as inform the lay reader. Budge had performed group workings with the Ka-Statue of Prince Setne Khamuast, whose name Set-Is-Kind A-Power-Is-Recognized-In-Thebes, shows his own alliances. Budge had spelled the name of the dawn god partially in Greek and Roman characters (X-e-φ-e-ρ). When Aquino invoked the Prince of Darkness on the night of North Solstice in the 1975 to ask for wisdom, the CHI (= X) flooded him. He was it as the Roman X, which equaled the Year (X Ae.S) as well marked him as the tenth Magus (using Crowley's Magi list). Aquino had resigned from the Church of Satan on June 10, X eleven days before he invoked the Prince of Darkness. Such floods of information are part of the contemplation of Self, which goes beyond conventional language. Such "magical" communication is difficult to describe to those, who have not experienced it.

Aquino's subjective universe was changed forever, as is anyone's who contemplates Being. His long and painful journey to found the

Temple of Set, would take its own book to describe (and given the shy and quiet nature of Dr. Aquino may not be seen in the outer world).

The Word of Being and Becoming has clarified the internal processes of many in the years that have followed. It is not an easy Word – it takes a great of deal of training to manage the contemplation of Being and not pigeonhole it into a conventional religious experience. It takes a good deal of courage and energy to pursue the path of Becoming that your Being demands. Then it takes courage to risk the bliss of Being again, for even though it will be enhanced, it will bring you the news that more Becoming is needed.

Yet it is the unstoppable Pulse of the universe of thinking beings. As you set reading this book, you are a long way from the home of a 29 year old stock broker in Santa Barbara, California. It's been a awhile since Nixon and Watergate. But part of the Pulse is in your hands now with its possibilities for bliss and hard work.

One may still profit by contemplating the X of Xeper – it is the crossroad of Being and Becoming, the real cross road where the Devil is invoked.

VII. Other Words

The Word of Xeper came into being in the matrix of other ideas, and has spawned other ideas. The Temple of Set recognizes some of these other ideas as important tools in Becoming. (Being needs no tools as it is beyond words). Any non-destructive tool a Setian uses for her Becoming is sacred to that Setian, and recognized by the Temple as her right. However certain tools are Recognized by the Temple. Let's look at the meaning of "Recognition" and then at five words: Thelema, Indulgence, Rûna, Remanifestation and Arkte. I'll end this essay by considering a word once active in the Temple : Xem.

Anton LaVey described "recognition" as one of the four needs of the black magician – along with wealth, wisdom and followers. He said that modern man aches for recognition, people knowing who he was and what he had done. He saw magic as a means of achieving recognition – of being center stage so that you could change world. Recognition kept you from having a soulless unhappy existence. It was a key to obtaining strength, wisdom and immortality. By letting your inner world know that you had friends in the outer world, the inner world would be inspired to be friends with itself (the great goal of Anton's word of Indulgence see below).

The Temple of Set sees Recognition as a medium for a deeper exchange than is possible by simple modes of communication. Recognition consists of seeing the Being inherent in another person, thing or idea. It means that the psyche has been alerted by the intellect to be open to certain phenomena. Recognition is the basis of the Temple of Set. In a group where anti-authoritarianism is expected and anti-nomianism a virtue, there can be no exchange unless individuals can obtain the right of respect. But there is a magical aspect to this, just as someone may desire to be Recognized as a Priest of Set, they are also open to the magic of the psyches so Recognizing them. This goes beyond the simple human concept of showing respect to those you govern. It means that you connect self to the group will, while still retaining your individuality.

Words may be Recognized as well as humans. If the Council of Nine so Wills a Word may be held as a model and tool for all Setians. This action is more than a simple recommendation, it is a affirmation that not only will this Word lead to Becoming, but that by enacting it you will generate material that will be useful to your fellow Setians. It means that by accepting/contemplating the Word you further other Setians in intangible ways as well.

Thelema— Θελημα. Aleister Crowley began his magical career with three things on his side. The first was an incredibly repressive childhood religion to revolt against, the second was a fine education perfectly located in time and space of his needs and the third was a Left Hand Path society called the Golden Dawn. The childhood religion gave him a Name – he was so wicked surely that he must be the Beast 666. When he was able to free himself from the guilt and oppression his psyche was able to send a powerful call into the universe for something else. His education in French literature gave his subconscious powerful tools to play with – such as the motto of the Abbey of Theleme "Do what thou wilt." Rabelais' utopian colony in *Gargantua and Pantagruel*. He lived at a time that the wealth of Eastern thought was just becoming available to the West, the magical culmination of the work of the Knights Templar. His psyche opened the mysterious doors that lead him to the Hermetic Society of the Golden Dawn. He was disappointed with their first lecture – on the Hebrew world AL אל . Later this became the key to his own work. The Golden Dawn taught that man could evolve through his own efforts, and that those efforts were enhanced by using magical methods of various sorts as focusing devices. When his need grew strong enough he was able to invoke Horus, who gave him the word of expansion "Thelema." Thelema is straightforward and misunderstood word. Its Cosmic purpose is to push man beyond the endless repeating cycle of existence symbolized by Osiris, the dying god. Its human purpose is to let individuals know that they call upon a hidden but active part of themselves to guide and energize their lives. The method of calling on this "higher self" is three fold – breaking with the norms of society so that the energy that keeps you fragmented can be used for your own purposes and not a purpose forced upon you, secondly by constantly seeking to find and refine this purpose through altering consciousness, and thirdly to understand that this process has always gone on producing the great men and women of history. Crowley had seen this process as ideally taking place in a fraternal brotherhood, which could provide assistance at all levels to the seeker. His Word produced several groups that have refined it. It can be found in the OTO, in modern Wicca, in the

German F.S., in the drug movement (Crowley introduced Huxley to mescaline), and in most of the positive material coming out of the Sixties. It captures all that is (from a Setian point of view) good in Horus. It is the embryonic form of Xeper. Crowley assumed that the self and universe were the same. He could not distinguish between the subjective and objective universe – or of you speak the language of the Quabala Thelema = 93, Thelema plus Self 25 = Xeper 118.

For the Setian Thelema is a simple map. Find out who you are, and then configure your inner and outer life to fulfill that knowledge. Crowley was a Utopian. He believed that if everyone found their Will – society would transform itself into a perfect world. He was a deeply moral and caring man. His concept of dedication is lost on most occultists who can not conceive of a lifework and are uninterested in magic when it fails to get them minor wishes they feel are true desires. His Word is a map.

From a completely different moral viewpoint comes Anton Szandor LaVey, a misanthrope, who Uttered the Word Indulgence in 1966 – year I of our Aeon. Indulgence is the word of the unified, and therefore powerful, psyche. Let say you are typing on your manuscript but you know your favorite pie (buttermilk) is in the refrigerator. It has power over you. You keep thinking about it, you hurry though your work or you decide to "tough it out" thinking about the pie every minute. Your psyche is not unified. LaVey noticed that the control structures of human society keep people from having unified psyches, and being in the thrall of whomever controlled the symbols of their desires. Want to get laid, but you're too ugly/shy/inept with women – then buy a car advertised by beautiful women draped over it. LaVey thought that human independence comes from discovering what turns you on and possessing it – either objectively or subjectively. The psyche with its wants fulfilled is powerful. No one can threaten it, tempt it, or make it feel bad. The symbol of the fulfilled psyche is Satan, and the human desire to feel recognition for its uniqueness in the Cosmos is what calls Satan to us. LaVey's system revolves around building closed environments, ritual chambers, and enacting one's desires. His magical methodology entered directly into Setian practice.

LaVey's Cosmos was one of cellars and hidden chambers all mimicking the Man Downstairs, the Principal of shutting one's self away in artificial paradises that influences the rest of the world by the magical link. As such he was drawn to French esotericism which had a fascination with shapes and containers, as well as accounts of Yezidi magical towers where Melek Taus was worshipped. He did not envision his teaching as creating anything other than a personal expression. He did not plan for the creation of the Church of Satan, nor once it was founded for a degree system within. He accepted these suggestions from others, but his own passion was for a closed off world. His Work continues in the world in his writings and the various Churches of Satan.

For us it is a beginning because it establishes two things: the notion that a unified psyche withdrawn from the world can create magical change and that the archetype of the Devil is the key to understanding the finite god who shaped our consciousness. Because of these two breakthroughs we (meaning both humans and Set) date our Aeon from this man's work, while ignoring his flaws that kept him from being active in the world. He lacked the moral edge of Crowley and the desire to interact with the objective universe that creates the true magician.

Nine years after Anton's Word another Word was Heard. (It was also eighteen years after Gregor A. Gregourius had introduced rune-work into the Fraternitas Saturni, a Left Hand Path groups– one of the more recent meetings of Set and Odhinn). Stephen Edred Flowers had been interested in the dark and mysterious all of his life. He had even joined the Church of Satan, getting a spooky looking membership card for his efforts, and a getting to read a few anonymous essays in the *Cloven Hoof* which Edred would later learn had been penned by Michael Aquino. Edred had decided on a career in journalism since he liked poking into things, and when he was 21 he was dragged along to meet a "Tibetan master" a disappointing, but amusing quest. As his friends drove back to Austin, Texas Edred heard a word "Roonah." So his quest began leading to his Utterance of the law *Reyn til Rûna!*, which the Temple of Set recognized as a V° word in the midsummer of XXV, sixteen years later. *Reyn til Rúna*, "Seek the Mysteries!" suggests a direction for the Will. On a Cosmic level, the human (Horian) universe is not to be randomly expanded by Will, but it is to be expanded based on Hidden information both within and without the Seeker. The deep quest for self-knowledge that can be explored through Crowleyan methods only works if friction and struggle complement the inner quest. This friction is based on seeking after hidden things in the objective universe which give the hidden inner self a vocabulary of words and images to express itself. Edred's Word came at a crucial time in his academic career. He was able to see that seeking the hard facts in the objective universe would require hard research, not fantasy and wild speculation. His methods often used academic research, language learning, travel and bodily ordeals. He began a year of intense magical workings to prepare for his life work. Some of these workings no doubt let the door open for Runic fakirs of various sorts, but they also seemed to effected the readings of Magister Caverni Michael Aquino, who far away in Kentucky began looking at the face behind Satan, and "randomly" found items such as the Xeper formula. The Old Norse sentence *Reyn til Rúna* written in its proper letters, the sixteen character Younger Futhark is ᚱᛂᛁᚾ ᛏᛁᛚ ᚱᚢᚾᛆ. By rune-tally this phrase is equal to 93. (The Younger Futhark was created by Runemasters to preserve and allow for the Remanifestation of Runic practices—for details see *Runes and Magic* by S. E. Flowers).

Nine years after Edred Heard Rûna, a crises was occurring in the Temple of Set. High Priest Ronald K. Barrett had left (see Xem below) and a fairly undignified power struggle was occurring. Michael Aquino had returned to the High Priesthood and was faced with a problem. If Setians were more evolved by the word of Xeper, why did they still act like jerks? (Most Magi die before seeing this part of their Work). He went to the Hall of the Dead in Himmler's Castle to ask the question. Why there? It is the cosmic symbol of lofty ambitions mixed with human evil. Why do humans fail? Aquino received his VI° Word "Walhalla." This word often rendered in the Temple as "Life" is a mediation about the nature of Loki, whose name means "Ender," and Odhinn, whose name means "Master of Inspiration." The "Ender" part of psyches causes eras to end in our lives and in the world. It shows up and wipes things away – using the very forces that built the things to start with. Aquino understood that Ragnaroks are inevitable, and that the way around them are magical enclosures of souls dedicated to making sure the next remanifestation is better. He copied Odhinn's method by creating the Order of the Trapezoid. He decided the OTR should study Lovecraft, Crowely, Runes and Nazi occultism. A few weeks later Edred, who knew nothing of this, had discovered the name of the Temple of Set, and that its head was his old mentor. He sent a letter in asking for admission and discussing his line of study, which although well known now, was unpublished then. The relationship between Xeper and Rûna was re-enacted (much as it had been between List's Word of Rune and Crowley's Word of Thelema).

When Edred joined the Temple, he brought an interest in scholarly research, hard data and lifetime commitment that was to change Temple practice. He fulfilled the Need Aquino had sensed. Edred had already founded the Rune Gild (1980), which is the field of his work and the appropriate place to seek after his Word. Six years after joining the Temple, Edred found an arrogant, fat and lazy pupil at his door named Don Webb, who used his methods to approach some Egyptian mysteries much as Michael Aquino had and found new gold. Edred's Word is the way out of the mud of occultism, and the idea that reconciles the needs of inner and outer worlds. It comes from the Age of Satan when Horus and Set ruled jointly, and will be the key for Setians to learn to reintegrate their Work into world, much as Indulgence is the key for breaking away.

Each Word is much more than meets the eye. The way the word comes into the world is a key to understanding it. In the middle of ritual Magister O. asked Magister James A. Lewis about what came beyond death – how would we remanifest? The question revealed a law of the universe to James A. Lewis. Remanifestation resolves the difference between Being and Becoming. It exists at all levels of the universe. It can be the simple remanifestation that every magician experiences of creating a subjective state inside the ritual chamber and then experiencing it as an objective change in the outer world. It is the change that can take what you learned in elementary school and make it show up in the fall in middle school. It is the principle of changing form while expressing Form, or of Reawakening after Sleep. Here would an example of form expressing Form – the sea pounds endlessly against a rock and makes sand. The sand, tiny and particulate, is the remanifestation of the rhythm of water. Here would be an example of Reawakening – after years you suddenly Understand a moment of blinding Truth you had as a child. You can't believe that you had forgotten. Of course the Truth is different now, now you have greater resources to act upon it. Remanifestation is the law that things return, and if you are prepared you can take advantage of their return – if it is a bad habit returning you can be ready to dampen or loose it, if it is a bad person you can be prepared to deal with him appropriately. If it is a good moment, such as a realization you can be ready to write it in your journal or to act on it. The human psyche will likewise return. Not reincarnate, but return in another form – just as your revelation did, or your magic did, or the waves did as sand. This word both explains the sense of cosmic familiarity we feel without using reincarnation, and gives us the challenging notion that although nothing in the universe is final we can learn to be better players. This word both curbs enthusiasm, and installs Hope. It is expressed in James Lewis' law: "Xeper and Remanifest." This is the law that is clumsily understood as karma. This word both explains what fetters you, and gives you the notion that planning, timing and will can free you from any bond. This Word provides the mechanism not only for my reUtterance of Xeper, but for future reUtterances as well. Thus the ability of the Temple to bring "fresh fever from the skies" is assured.

The relationship of soul life to body life has an especial interest to the Western Left Hand Path. We do not shun, abhor, or believe the body to be an illusion. We think the key to an aware and powerful soul life is found in the body. This idea has been cooking for sometime. It began when Magister Aquino wrote the Induction rite for the Louisville Grotto of the Church of Satan. Initiates pledged to accept the "pains and pleasures of existence" (perhaps a little of Aquino's search through existentialism showing here) and to make a bond with the paws that had trod the "pure pagan silt." Anton LaVey slightly rewrote this rite and made it into the "Adult Satanic Baptism" found in the *Satanic Bible*. This rite with its combination of accepting life and honoring biological life was the root of much more thinking. When then Magistra Lilith Aquino and Magister O. founded the Order of the Vampyre (OV) they began to explore the secret doors between body and soul. The OV came to explore shamanism and dance, with a particular interest in shape shifting. Lilith and her students began to feel a sympathy to those animals whose forms they borrowed magically. It's not easy to be a wolf one night and read about the destruction of their homes in the newspaper the next day. This feeling grew into a passion, which began to express itself in all aspects of Maga Aquino's life, eventually leading her to form an element dedicated to Understanding animal life and protecting it. In seeking a Name for the group she asked her fellow Masters. I had been magically experimenting with the name Arktê Αρκτη, which Edred had suggested to her as the proper form of the bear goddess mentioning in the magical papyri. She choose this name for Arkte's Avengers, and the Name began to open internal doors. It provided a compliment to the word of Walhalla uttered eighteen years before. It emphasized that one of the ways not to succumb to the distractions of the life process was to exalt the Life process. To actually feel the cosmic pulse as your own pulse, to see the mysteries that are found in all human flesh, to love the Earth that was called into being to house Xeper – all of these things seemed well symbolized by the Bear Goddess who turns the spindle of fate. Like Lord Loki, she brings all things to an end. She brought her Word to my attention in the Year XXXV, and I carried to the Council of Nine for Recognition.

These words are the stars that guide us now. Others will Come Into Being, as our process produces Magi. Like the tribe of ancient Persia called the Magush, whose name gave us "magic" or the ancient Germanic tribe the Eruli, the Temple of Set is the tribe of ritual specialists for the world.

The Word Xem, pronounced Khem, had as its ur-form the Word Al-Khemi Uttered by René Schwaller de Lubicz. In 1917, he had received his magical name of Aor, and an impulse to discover the meaning of the name. *Aor* is "light" in Hebrew," but "inheritance" in Egyptian. He was a student of Alchemy, and his quest lead him to certain experiments which provided him the following insights: the Objective Universe can be manipulated to discover truths about the subjective universe, the quest of manipulation (with its hardships) purifies the seeker so that the outer truths will appear at the correct times for the individual to further his evolution; the seeds for evolution are already inside of the self and may reveal themselves to you in the form of a Name. His work in the early part of the twentieth century especially with his colleague Fulcanelli) thoroughly colored French esotericism leading ultimately to texts like *The Morning of the Magicians* and *Houses that Kill*, which were major sources for LaVey. His quest lead him to Egypt, where he found in ancient Egyptian civilization a paradigm for his process. He was fascinated with four ideas. One that you could you have a civilization that could provide the outer quest (in the form of temple building) to match the inner one, so that it would create its own philosopher kings. Two that gods, in Egyptian *Neteru*, were human constructions just like the temples made from careful observation of the human psyche and continuously improving as Initiates rose to their level and manifested their Name. Three that human beings had an Inheritance that made these things possible. Four that you could receive guidance from that Inheritance both as a word/name/symbol and a magical power to draw certain experiences to you. He symbolized each of these ideas with words taken from his reading of the works of Wallis Budge, that Golden Dawn initiate who had willed an Egyptian Remanifestation and gave us the unusual spelling of Xeper.

For the notion of a magical community he chose Amon-Re, the Neter of rulership. "Amon," the Hidden, is coupled with Re, the manifest. The King is the one who joins inner and outer lives so well that he can help others find their inner quests and provide their outer ones. (This notion still lives on French esotericism.) The gods were referred to by Budge's spelling of *Neteru*, which actually was probably pronounced "Nadjerruu," — a divine community could exist for people at the end of their Initiation, which would mirror their true natures as seen by the King. The process by this was called Khem, which he believed to be the root of the word "alchemy" (actually alchemy comes from a Chinese word meaning to make gold, via Syrian, the people they bought mercury from). Khem both means to "make perfect" used for pottery firing, teaching children and the process of addition and "ignorance." One passed and suffered through ignorance until its fire perfected you. The notion of inheritance was "Aur" the Egyptian word that means both Thigh and Inheritance and matches Schwaller's name. As a child of the gods, one would return to the gods. (This notion in French esotericism has been debased into countless UFO cults). The seven stars called the Thigh of Set, which we call the Big Dipper or the Great Bear, was the center of the night sky. The last notion, the Word, he referred to as Medu Neter, which means the Words of the Gods, which is what the Egyptians called their Hieroglyphs. Schwaller expressed his teaching in a series of books which dominated the French esoteric scene in the sixties and began appearing in English in the seventies.

Meanwhile a young Thelemite named Ronald Keith Barrett knew nothing of this. In 1966 he sought illumination using Crowley's methods. He received a magical book called the *I AM PAPERS,* which had the notions of the Unknown but guiding Name and the idea of a divine inheritance. He followed these mysteries to the door of the Church of Satan. He looked like a good candidate to Anton, he ran an occult bookstore in New York City and he had a beautiful assistant, who would later take the name of Lilith (see Arkte above). When Set founded his Temple, Barrett followed Aquino seeing the same voice in the *Book of Coming Forth by Night*, that had spoken to him ten years before. In the Temple of Set he met Magistra T.B., who introduced him to Schwaller's writings. He found the language of his revelation and Schwaller became a pillar for Setian understanding – *Her Bak* being almost required reading for Setians for years.

He Uttered Xem in the Year XV. It had certain flaws. Initiation doesn't happen like story-books. The inner life of a human and the outer life don't run on parallel tracks. No one can look at a person and say what their quest should be. The names of gods are not maps for how people fit together. The notion of a magical civilization ruled by an all wise king didn't translate into a group that had broken with society to proclaim friendship with the Prince of Darkness. The real world overcame the fantasy world. Several of the truths of Xem remain in the Temple, but two truths overcame its rule: You can't give someone the outer quest that prepares them for the inner revelation. People have to find their quest.

You can't give people the inner revelation, only they can find it by discovering their own resonance with the source of their divine inheritance.

VIII. The Degree System and the Structure of the Temple

The Temple of Set possesses a degree system. Setians regard these degrees as objective descriptions of states of being, and think that having such states recognized by others is an aid both to the people so Recognized and to running the objective manifestation of Set' Temple. Since so many of my essays as High Priest made reference to these degrees I will expand upon the Temple's reasons for using a degree system, the degrees themselves and conclude with some remarks about the structure of the Temple.

People seek Initiation for two reasons. On one hand, people who don't fit in are looking for a peer group. This means that every new religion, political party or occult group will be filled with misfits, hungry for basic human recognition. The group can enforce its values by rewarding those who fit in with titles and responsibility. Pride, the invention of Lucifer, does nicely as a motivator until something better comes along. On the other hand, people seek Initiation as a means of obtaining tools to enhance or discover themselves and need feedback from other humans about their achievements. These two forces combine in the degree system to ensure that the Temple produces its own teachers and will be a self-sustaining system. In Temple terminology the degree system would be a magical Working – it attracts the elements it needs, transforms them, and causes the transformed elements to work on the world-at-large changing and conditioning it to provide better and better elements to feed the on-going process. It has aspects of all three sorts of Black Magic – Lesser Black Magic (LBM) using human pride and the lure of the forbidden to draw people into the Temple (as well as assuring that such small group receives a large amount of press), Medial Black Magic (MBM) by effecting the environment through synchronicity and sorcery so that the Temple appears to the right people at the right times, and that the initiates of the temple are protected from many of the hostile forces of the world so they can pursue the delicate work of self-change and lastly Greater Black Magic (GBM) so that the people can achieve self-actualization by learning the unique laws of their own beings. The degrees of the Temple are six: Setian, Adept, Priest/Priestess,

Magister/Magistra, Magus/Maga, Ipsissimus/Ipsissima. These grades are influenced by the grade system of the Golden Dawn (and more remotely by the grade system of European trade guilds), but I would like to focus on the Temple's meaning of them.

The **Setian I°** is a grade of willed reception. Long before anyone enters the Temple of Set, they undergo the experience of discovering that they **can** be responsible for their coming into being. They are faced with the knowledge of the many forces that have shaped them, and they make the decision to take control of as many of these forces as possible. This revelation and revolution effect things on many levels. The first is sense of anger at the world. How could the forces of the human world produce so much poison? The thought processes are like the rebellion of Satan in Judeo-Christian mythology, or the shock that placed the Buddha on his path to enlightenment. It is not intellectual or "deep" but it is powerful. The emotional break provides tremendous energy for the new initiate – the emotional fuel that they had used for years to make the inner world match the outer one, is now used to strengthen and heal the inner world. To people watching them, they may look like adults reliving their teenage years (the biological time when energy is made available to the inner world). To themselves they suddenly seem sane – suddenly full of the idea of making themselves whole and strong. This change of their subjective universes produces a change in the objective universe. The Temple of Set appears to them in a mysterious fashion. Suddenly a sense that previously had helped them navigate their psyches, lets them see the existence of a resonate set of people in the outer world. If they pass the admissions criteria, they are given access to two sorts of learning. They can read about philosophical and magical practices that if applied can help them quicken the awakening process that they have already started in their own selves. Likewise they are allowed to find III° mentors that can offer them questions that help them decide what to change, strengthen and explore about themselves. The magical force that allowed them to find the Temple will link them up with mentors who are dealing with the same issues from a place of having been transformed by the Temple's teaching. This allows for rapid personal development in a magical context. Success for the I° is the understanding that a full life comes from learning the habits of skepticism, philosophical inquiry, magical practice and finding that both allows them to be cut off from the mind-numbing aspects of the world while providing a community of fellow seekers. Failure for the I° can come in two ways. He may forget the truth that he needs to be Receptive to those things in the universe that are helpful (or he forgets that it is hard work to be Receptive), or he forgets that there is a blend of both the rational and the supra-rational in life. With all degrees the success or failure is a lifetime affair, if people loose contact with their "beginner's mind" their Initiation ends.

The Adept II° is a degree of willed transmission. The Adept has awakened to a couple of intense magical truths. The first is that the universe is run by magic. The out-pouring of the human will for millennia is what sustains and expands the universe. It is both within and outside of the adept herself. It may show up in an impulse to buy a certain sort of soft drink, or having the opportunity to change the policy of her university. People are both the commander and tool of an impersonal force, and the Adept learns that her own sendings can begin to make her more of a commander. The second truth that the Adept learns is that she is not her sendings. There is a difference between the self and its actions. One does not become more vast by doing a great deal of magic, nor do things begun by a person belong to or obey that person. Actions have consequences, but actions do not make the Self – rather they set up for the Self to discover the Self. There is great freedom and power in these ideas. The energy released here is self-created, not merely a redirection of energy away from the universe and toward the inner self. This degree is the most fun degree. The Adept is not drawn magically toward her mentors, but seeks them out. She will find the Masters more comforting. The Masters have formed an approach to the universe in a form of structured Play, which complements the Work the Adept is setting up for with her sendings into the Universe. The Adept may fail in two ways. The most likely is not focusing their new found freedom – they become the pawns of the occult industry trying this or that as long as the pickings are easy. The rarer form of failure is ego-inflation. The initiate comes to believe that no one else has ever had the synthesis that he or she has. The over-enthused one will break off and found her own organization, which (although a tad diluted) serves the future of the Aeon. Success for the Adept is discovering life-work – something that benefits themselves and their folk and keeps them interested and productive for their whole lives. If all human beings could reach the grade of Adept, the world would be transformed into a Paradise.

But for some there is a need to go beyond the first two levels. They have awakened to life, and they have separated their day-to-day selves from their eternal selves – learning to use the former to express the later. But they want to change themselves in deeper ways. They seek the purification of the fires of Set. They have deep issues they want to change in themselves and they need help to do so. They send their wills across the dark angles of space and time until they find Set. Set made a pact with mankind in 1966 (or as we say, Year I, AS), and that pact was that he would share of his Essence. The Adept, who has learned the art of having his day-to-day self express his eternal self, can allow his day-to-day self to express Set as well. He becomes open to a great power. He is not lost in that power, but if his sense of self is strong – he can use that power to restructure himself. Think of a teaspoon of salt in a glass as your eternal self. Adding water to the glass does not change the salt. It is still there although it components interact with each other and the rest of the world rather differently. Then if you evaporate the water, the salt remains (perhaps slightly increased and modified by the salts in the water), but it has a new configuration. This is like the encounter with Set, that the III° has. They are the cups of brine. Change seems instant, and their Intent of Purification draws others seeking the same process. First degrees from all over the planet will write them, friends at their work seek them out, family members, ho have never given them the time of day need their words. The advice, meditations and experiments they can suggest for others are also exactly what they need. This is the Daath of the Quabalists. The Priest or Priestess has no need for human initiators at this point, but instead advisors who are veterans of this state of consciousness. Hence the Priest develops strong ties with a Master, usually the one whose Order he had joined during his second Degree. Since the Priest has passed through the first two states, he is able to Recognize them. It is his job to aid the First Degree to awaken and begin the alchemical processes of the Second Degree. Since the Priest has become an expression of the Will of Set, he is a living incarnation of Set, a Temple of Set. Because of this internal fact, the not-for-profit corporation of the Temple of Set belongs to its Third Degrees. The Priest of or Priestess may fail in two ways. The energizing of his many components may unbalance him leading him to excesses of the Will ranging from moral indignation ("I'm a better Priest than these bums!") to the sense of being above other humans in ethical choices ("Stop lights are for other people!"). The success of the Priest is measured in both magical effects relating to the Priesthood (for example the archives of a hitherto almost unknown Left Hand Path Brotherhood are given to him) and acts of *realmagie*, he is able to give lecture about the Left Hand Path at colleges and universities. The effort at being one's self in the greate stream of Power that comes forth from Set is tough. It purifies and strengthens the self, and ends the fight of the many little wills, the many "I's" that Gurdjieff speaks of.

For fewer still another plain opens. If the Priestess has remained her basic self and admits the storm of Set, she can reverse the process of the Second Degree. Instead of separating the day-to-day self from the Eternal self, so that the former expresses the latter – she can unite these halves. Every action in her day-to-day life is at perfect harmony with the eternal life. This is a state of Mastery. Here the Initiate radiates out a calmness, for they are nourished by their subjective universes, and constantly calm and nourish the objective universe by their Being. At this level, called **Magister/Magistra IV°**, the lessons of the three degrees are synthesized and returned to the universe in the form of a teaching. The need to withdraw from the matrix of stupidity and pursue an ethical and exciting life of the First Degree lives in the Fourth by the latter's need for energy to maintain their equilibrium. The Second Degree's quest for life-work is one of the major chemicals of the Fourth Degree's alchemy. The Fourth Degree is pursuing the life-work found in the Second Degree, and benefiting from the hard work done then. The Third

Degree's secret of expressing the Will of Set while not loosing one's self is needed even more as a unified self is the unit of expression, not merely a self created by Initiatory will. These three needs are answered by actions cast in the world. The Fourth Degree will have spent most of her adult life in the Temple, and is synthesizing the day-to-day self and the eternal self while using the flowing Will of Set as a source for energy for her task. The Fourth Degree expresses this joint Will in an Order – a unified place of teaching. The harmony of the Order attracts certain Second Degrees because it gives them an objective touchtone for their self-exploration. Since the Fourth Degree is an ordered Being, the remanifestation of their Being in the world is an ordered Being. From them the living Aeon flows and works upon the world. It is therefore from their ranks the Council of Nine is Chosen. The Fourth Degree may fail in two ways. She may be overcome by the tranquility of her own synthesis and simply stop acting. She will painlessly pass back to the Sleep she came from (unless she had set certain magics in place as a Second Degree to awaken her). Or she may balk at the hard work of deep self exploration and decide that she does not want to unify herself and would prefer the artificial state of Being called the Third Degree. The Fourth Degree's success is found in the impact her Order makes on the Aeon, and the impact she makes on the world around her. Since she has passed through the previous three states it is her job to help people passing from the Second to the Third Degree.

The above are the human grades of the Temple. They may be summarized alchemically: enliven the metal, separate the volatile form the fixed, cleanse the body, restore the volatile to the fixed.

If the answer to the Master IV°'s question, "What over-reaching theme in my life made my synthesis possible?" **and** the answer to the Aeon's question "What aspect of Becoming is most needed for the evolution of myself?" is the same Principle, the Master is transformed by Remembering his Word. He becomes a **Magus V°** and his Task is to spread his Word. The Word of a Magus is partially known to his conscious self and partially hidden in the future actions of theirs. So he must preach this Word to the world in as many ways he can. All that Hear his Word are profited thereby, even if they do not wholly accept it. Since it is a magical utterance it effects all of humankind to some degree. However if the Magus can not cause enough people to Hear the Word (in other words to be as receptive to it as a First Degree is receptive to the wisdom they seek), the Magus fails. Words clear areas for themselves. They create meso-cosmoi to incubate in, they create odd channels to live and remanifest through, the create support structures in advance of their coming so that they might thrive. Most of what people who are "into the occult" study is how words live. For their meso-cosmoi they study conspiracy theory, for their odd paths they study synchronicities (without asking themselves why-and-how these things develop), for the coming into being of support structures they develop simplistic beliefs in hypnosis and mass belief. Words are not made powerful by the number of people that "believe" in them, but the quality of minds that work to refine them. One does not come closer to a Word by discovering its magical powers of manifestation but by applying it to one's life. The Magus will fail if he does not grasp this. If he feels that the Word will do the work, he fails because he does not get to receive the illumination of the Word in the works of others. The Fifth Degree is about Reception, not the initial reception of the Word from the Prince of Darkness, who told you to "Remember!" but the reading of the living book that others create from what you have shared. Fifth Degrees fail if they think the work of others "belong" to them, because they Uttered the Word. They succeed if they approach the actions of others who have Heard their word using the lessons of the previous four degrees.

The last degree the Temple of Set Recognizes is that of **Ipsissima VI°**, "the very own self." The Temple originally called this degree Rex/Regina, which I personally prefer. The Maga has gathered the greatest Secret. She sees how the principle that ruled her Becoming works in a universal way – not in a personal way, not in a theoretic way – but in objectively observable ways. This knowledge frees her psyche from the particulars of her incarnation. In a real sense her outer life is now a mask or an illusion – an eidolon for other incarnated beings who seek understanding. This state has certain peculiarities, since the Knowledge of her Principle is in everything she does, anything that she can get started in the world becomes self-sustaining because it carries her Word within it. This does not mean she has any earlier time starting things than any human, it merely means that she can create eternal things in the world of becoming. This power is constrained in an understanding of balance. She can not give too much, because if she makes it too easy, others will not traverse the road. So her challenge is to find ways to make her Work contact and interact with the work of others before her – just as she has found proof that her work is universal, she must give that proof back to the Cosmos. If she fails in this exchange she looses the benefits of living. It is not enough to be eternal, only a living potent immortality is of interest to the followers of the Left Hand Path.

I have presented these Degrees as a simple linear path. As with anything involving human consciousness the rules are never simple. The eternal part of a human exists outside of both cyclic and linear time and is Working to some extent in all of these areas. The human recognition of these states helps the Initiate to find the best work for the time of his life.

IX. The Future of the Aeon

By the Will of the Masters, the Aeon has Come Into Being.

It bears the stamp of each man and woman that has willed it into Being.

It is not a robot, a golem, or a computer program. It is self-willed.

Its highest and purest form of expression is the Temple of Set, where Initiation passes and evolves through a living human system. After this its next highest form are those organizations and philosophies that have been called into existence for the word Xeper's home. Most of these, such as freedom movements in cyber-space or school of optimal psychology don't look in the least bit magical.

The next layer of manifestation are the written and spoken works of Temple members. After this comes the groups founded by ex-Setians and those occult groups effected by our Word.

As predicted in the *Book of the Law*, the eighties were a bad time for Becoming. As representatives of the Prince of Darkness, the Temple and its Teachings were the perfect paper tigers to attack. Although Judeo-Christian ethics (in fact any kind of ethics) has ceased to rule the world – superstition and prejudice remained and flourished. The temple was directly attacked by governments, media and large corporations, yet we remained and grew slowly. Truth is a powerful weapon and can even get though times of no money.

There are about to be some changes in the Aeon's manifestation. With a good deal of witch-hunting gone, several small groups have sprung up putting forth their own watered down synthesis of the Aeon, so there is active recruiting on a popular level. Some of the people so touched will seek out better sources. The patient approach the Temple has always had toward serious academics has gained us a niche in the thinking world, so that we can participate in the larger marketplace of ideas. The world is becoming aware of the matrix of stupidity – even movies and talk shows now discuss ideas once found only in Plato. There will be more people entering into the Aeon, and of a higher quality. The Temple's careful building of infrastructure will come into play.

This means new questions can finally be addressed.

What does Initiation mean as a lifetime pursuit? For the first forty years of the Aeon we have mainly turned out Adepts who have returned to the world when the novelty of occult practice failed, or the social strain of being a member of a "Satanist" group was too great. What will it mean when we have hundreds of Masters rather than 20? What can we discover about Initiation for the 70 year old, the 80 year old, etc.

What does it mean when we begin making more and more of our own tools? Currently we use the tool sets a large number of occult and philosophical systems – how will things change when we have produced enough quality material so that new Initiate grows up on our words, field-tested on our own processes? Or in other words what happens than the Aeon has the same state as the VI°?

What does it mean when we are no longer an American centered group? We have grown a great deal beyond California of the mid-seventies. We have a significant number of Initiates all over the world. This also means we have more and more access to the secret traditions of other lands, and an even greater picture of the potentials for human awareness.

What does it mean when the skills we teach our Initiates – pattern recognition, timing, ability to immerse into other modes of thought without becoming (unwillingly) programmed by them, dreaming, and magic become the skills for dealing with ultra-rich information world? Words create worlds – whether it's John Dee's word of Dominion, which created the British Empire and the corporation or Plato's word of Remembering that created the possibility for non-culture based philosophic speculation – our Word is creating a world where our skills will shape the world. What will that world be like?

For you as you read my essays and discuss them with your tough-minded friends, there is one question. Do you want to work and help pull those answers out of the Neheh, the Darkness the profane call the Future? Or do you want to watch?

Notes from Neheh

Note One

Neheh (pronounced Neheck) is the Eternal Future waiting to be filled with deeds of Xeper. It is the great Darkness ruled by Set-Heh, the Eternal Set, and those who manifest His essence by deed and thought.

Concerning the High Priesthood By unanimous vote of the Council of Nine, I Don Webb, became the third High Priest of Set since the fall of pagan Egypt. That I have rather large shoes to fill is an understatement, that I have a better crew to work with and for and be aided by is likewise an understatement. The administration of the Temple will continue in the same pattern: administrative notes to the Executive Director, money to the Treasurer, and the rest of it to me.

The High Priest is not a being more sacred to, nor more important to, Set. Each Setian represents the possibility of a unique genius, a unique potential that can grow to be as Set. I trust that all of you treat each other with this wonder in mind. The High Priest's job is one of synthesis and communication of that synthesis in magical fashion to effect the principle tool of the Aeon, the Temple of Set. The High Priest must (try to)-synthesize the hungry excitement of the I°, the endless growing edge of the Temple that is the II°, the refining fire of human consciousness that is in the III°, the wisdom of the IV°, the clarity of the V°, and the elusive shine of the VI°. Where do I get these things for my synthesis? From the unique actions of every Setian arising in the context of this Temple that is their own continuous re-creation.

Concerning the Temple This historic year has seen a lot of changes in the human organization that reflects your Xeper. The human organization, a not-for-profit California-based corporation, reflects what is the best and the worst in the **real** Temple, the Temple you have built in your mind, soul, and body. There is a tendency to think that the Temple of Set is "out there" somewhere in Conclaves, newsletters, medallions. The Real Temple is sometimes neglected, because it is forgotten. With all the crackling energy of the Aeon's latest movements, it is a good time to find out what the state of the **real** Temple is. Where do things stand in your mind, your soul, your body? What maintenance needs to be done in these realms, so that you can manifest the godlike being which already exists implicitly in-your deepest levels of Being?

This is also a good time to figure out your relationship to the human organization. What is this group for, anyway? Is it a place you're planning to find in your next incarnation? Is it a fairly keen social club? Or is it (possibly) something much, much finer — if you Worked to bring it to a higher level of manifestation? Or is it all of these and more?

Concerning Orders The Temple is about to see the Order system reach a new level of strength and independence. Some of the Orders are turning very public faces to the world, such as the Order of the Trapezoid and the Vampyre. Some less directly such as the amazing efforts of the Order of Shuti.

In the Spirit of Working II, Orders will have a great deal more autonomy. This is not the Temple breaking up, but an example of the Temple fulfilling its Aeonic function. Orders represent communicable methods of Initiation. Each will grow to be more like itself with time. The job of Order members will be to stretch themselves in two directions. On one hand they will be on the experimental edge of the Order, on the other they will want to share the Order's fruits with the Temple in a plain and easy-to-grasp speech. Share what you know and your power will grow. Explain what your Order is about to members of your Pylon. If you have dual membership, explain the thinking and methods of each to each. Every Order member must plant his experience in the center of the Temple and on the cutting edge of their Order at the same time.

Concerning the Feminine The psyche has no gender. Let me say that again. The psyche has no gender. Expressions of the psyche can have gender. In all of our psyches there are both masculine and feminine Forms and forces. We haven't looked too closely at the feminine in the Temple, because the old models of the feminine prevalent in the occultnik world are so degrading to women. You can choose the OTO woman-is-whore or the Wiccan-woman-is-super-mom. In short the bad images of the world — basically infantile masculine fantasies — have been made sacred by the Right Hand Path.

Lets begin looking at aspects of the feminine that resonate with our sole goal, that of Xeper. I've had a great deal of help with finding these ideas especially from Priestess Q, Priestess O., Magister L., Magistra I., Priest T., Adept C. Priestess T., and Priestess Y. I'd like to to look at Set's three wives.

Nepthys's name is so holy that is was a cult secret. Neb-Thys merely means "Lady of the House." Her birth signified the beginning of time, her altars were the birthing beds, used so that the child might get a good *Ba* at birth. It is likely that her name was *Norea*, the name the Setian gnostics had for the female archetype. In the Egyptian language *Norea* means "Victory." (The First Beast identified the Greek goddess of Victory NIKH, with the number 93). Nepthys represents the goal, which when obtained leads to a higher level of being, plus having descendants on this earth to carry on the Work. She can be equated with the Ninth Angle/Black Flame. She isn't the nurturing of mom, but the nurturing that a dream of the future gives you.

Anat, the bisexual warrior goddess, came to Egypt with the Syrians. Her name means "foresight." Her qualities are great love for her mate, bloodthirstiness in battle, and above all the need for preparedness in battle.

Astarte, another Syrian goddess, was the protector of the Pharaoh's chariot. She is a form of Istar/Inanna, the archetype of the Scarlet Woman. She represents a perfect manifestation of the inner state — your "dream date" made flesh as it were. This goes far beyond sexual fantasies — she represents any desirable thing that magic has made manifest in the world.

Concerning Ra-En-Set. The question of how to honor Dr. Michael A. Aquino, is before us. What do you say to the man who brought down the fire from heaven?

There have been others who have held the Aspect of Ra-En-Set before Michael A. Aquino, I hold that Aspect as part of the Instrumentality of the High Priest. But there have been none before, nor will there be after any who can lay claim to the Name of Ra-En-Set: Michael Aquino Uttered the Eternal Word of Set in the manner that set him aside, and above all others before or to come.

The name Ra-En-Set shows up, as far as I know, only once. It is in the Pyramid texts. It is the Source of Healing for the damage done by Set. The damage done by Set, as we all know is his Gift. It turned us from happy monkeys to creatures with a desire for meaning, hence creatures with fear, misery, and anxiety. The Mouth of Set is the source of the piece of meaning that heals the soul, by telling the soul how it can heal itself. Ra-En-Set Uttered the Word that is the key to healing the existential dilemma of mankind. It brings access to a happiness that those not possessed of the Word cannot know. Yes, Virginia, there are emotional states that only the Children of Set can know — it is the heartfelt proof of our election. Setians have access to emotions and energies that others simply do not. It is the subjective proof, discovered though magical introspection, that shows we have Come Into Being at a more divine level than our fellows. There will be small tokens of our immense debt to Dr. Michael A. Aquino at Conclave, but those who feel the debt most sharply in their chest, will send their tokens to him long before. Let those who See what has been wrought, speak their hearts, write their poems, and do their magic to fill the life of this man with prosperity, health, wonder, and magic.

ON THE FOUR WORLDS

Most Setians live in four worlds. Some manage a fifth or sixth. In no particular order, I'll list them, and comment on Xeper in each.

1. The world of the body. Here is the great lusty engine that will carry you through as many adventures as you can conceive. Its maintenance is your first goal. Learn what diseases your family is subject to, and how to avoid them, learn how to exercise and eat, learn how to sleep. Your second goal is refining the body. Learn what pleasures it finds most keen, learn how to move with grace, learn how to adorn it. Your third goal is learning how to train your body— this can be yoga or martial arts or whatever depending on your genius. Here Xeper is possible. When you alter your physical make-up to better express your psyche, you are engaging in Xeper. Your fourth goal is altering the world, so that your body has a better chance of survival. This can mean anything from cleaning up pollution in your neck of the woods, to putting in security lights. As in the third goal, Xeper is possible here. The

body has a special chemistry, unique to your family and circumstance. Learn to use it. Learn to run around in your youth, learn to consolidate in your middle age, learn to distill in your old age. Watch those among your family and friends that have mastered these arts.

2. The world of what is already created and conditioned. This is the world that exists all around you, it doesn't care a fig if you died, and you have to reconfigure yourself to fit into it. It is the world of the job, the airport, the traffic jam. Here is the most resistant battlefield, and therefore the place the Setian can learn the most. Your first job here is to configure as many things as you can to give you happiness. Small victories count — getting a video store to change its rental policy, getting your dry cleaners to give out free candy — every day cause the world to render up a little more happiness for you. Your second job is to reconfigure things so that you will have more power. Now "more power" can mean more money, or more vacation time, or more of a hand in your company's policy. This is the same as all the work-a-day people around you. But you have an opportunity for Xeper, if you take the power in a manner that is awake and personal. Your third job is reconfiguring the world to reflect you. This might mean becoming the CEO, or getting your own business, or any of a thousand things. Again this is the same goal as the rest of the world, but it becomes your goal if pursued consciously. Goals like this take a long-time, they may start with going to law school tomorrow. Fourthly your job is to reconfigure the world, so that where ever you have been a greater opportunity for personal freedom is left behind. This isn't altruism, this is changing the world to reflect the conditions of your mind — it is Magical Objectivism (or Apollonian Satanism).

3. The world of personal choice. Here all things that are truly personal, such as your fantasies and your dreams, live. Here there is the least resistance, so little is learned, but there is the most freedom so many ideas can be tried out. Your first job is too separate out your day-dreaming and do it well. Most people daydream all the time at work and home — a sort of muddy self-comforting process. Set aside a time for your fantasies. Learn to be awake when you want to be awake, and lost in intense fantasy when you want that. Your second job is to objectify some of your fantasies. You must make some of them appear in the real world, see and touch and taste what has been only in your dreams. This might be called Dionysian Satanism. This practice of "making dreams come true" is a very important part of Xeper. It doesn't matter if it's sex or travel or gardening. Do it! See the results before you!

4. The world of the Aeon of Set. This world is partially internal to those who have succeeded in becoming Elect and partially external. Your first job is to explore the world of the Aeon in new ways. This can be writing to a Setian in another country, or seeking out a book in a Reading List topic that you know nothing about, or hosting a group of Setians at your home for magic and talk. Your second job is to protect

the Aeon. Now that can mean anything from being sure that your Temple materials are safe, to writing a letter to your newspaper about the nonexistence of so-called Satanic crime, to having a sincere heart-to-heart chat with a worried friend who doesn't know what to think of your dark side. Your third job is to enhance the world of the Aeon. You have unique intellectual and magical potentials that can't be expressed fully in the World of Horrors. You have things to say, that by the process of getting ready to say them, saying them, and getting feedback on them will contribute not only to our Temple, but to your Xeper. If you really want to learn a topic, try to teach it.

There's a twofold secret to dealing with these worlds. The first part is that we tend to ignore whatever world is bothering us the most, by doing too much in another. We get medallion-crazy when our business is on the skids, we neglect our health when we're too busy painting our fantasies in the studio. Find out how many worlds you live in — and then do something that reminds you to balance the activities. Don't put off going to school because you're writing too many Setians, don't put off answering your letters because you're not selling enough insurance policies. The second part is to learn how to get energy flowing from one world to another. This is an important part of the Royal Art of being more than you seem. An example would be discovering that your local community college has an "Introduction to Philosophy" course. Let's say you've always wanted to be a great thinker (World 3), well you've got to start somewhere. You call up your personnel office and ask if the company has any aid for people taking night classes (World 2) — and sure enough they don't have any money, but it does add to your performance review! Then you check the schedules and get a class three times a week — a twenty-minute bike ride from your house. Leave the car at home and work off that winter gut (World 1). After the course is over, give a talk about what you've learned to your Pylon (World-4). Now it's hard to find an example as perfect as this, but you can learn how to Xeper in all the aspects of your life, and how to move the resulting energy form aspect to aspect for greater happiness and power.

Note Two

Concerning the Religion of Osiris. The most popular religion of the world is the religion of Osiris, because it's the easiest. It is easy in that it requires no thinking. It may masquerade as Christianity or agnosticism or being a Republican or a Democrat or just watching *Larry King Live*. It has many masks, some of which a Setian could do as well (such as being a Republican or a Democrat). Its word is *Wen* or stasis, a word that is always an opposite of Xeper This religion can even give the semblance of Life, but causes its adherents to enact great patterned activity— usually by following its buzzwords. The Word of stasis has two very bad aspects for the Setian. Firstly it denies Xeper. Secondly it unites you to a collective. Let's look at each of those, since such a powerful word often hypnotizes us. To be Setian is not to worship Set but to love what Set loves, and hate what Set hates as a guideline to finding initiatory experiences. I assume you all know that Osiris and Set don't have a loving relationship.

It denies Xeper. The Osirian judges not from the direction that a person is heading, but from where the person has been. So it judges the highs or lows of a person's existence in historical time. If a person has been a movie star, then they're good. It doesn't matter if the person is currently in a decaying orbit of drugs and despair. If a person has been a wretched street criminal, then they're bad, it doesn't matter that they're on their way to Becoming a brilliant philosopher. The Osirian may believe in confession, but not in change. If he or she looks at anyone, it is as though they were looking at them at their moment of glory or infamy — it is simply too difficult to look at them in movement. This is also the source of what passes for self-knowledge in these people. They define themselves with the winning play in the High School football game twenty years ago (if they have a good self image), or with the bad divorce that they know is their fault (if they have a bad self image). Those with a bad self image tend to become psychic vampires, those with a good self image tend to become bigots (of all stripes). Such folk are gainfully avoided by the LHP practitioner. Gee, how easy life would be if I could only see myself at my best— but I am Cursed with the Black Flame. When I write about any Initiatory problems, it is not from the light of a refulgent black halo, but the occasional moment of clarity (or Sense of Xeper) that lets me see these things in myself — and that at my best I can put in motion changes within and without against these shortcomings.

Osirian thinking unites to a collective. The Osirian afterworld was a conscious denial of Self, and identification with Osiris, which led you to a changeless world — just like Egypt but without floods or drought. Every year just the same. The essence of the Left Hand Path is the quest for an **individual**, that is to say non-collective, immortality. Now our society is plagued by a collective search for identity — a search that allows people to have some outer force do the thinking for them. Any displacement of the body of the individual which leads to a primary identification with others is detrimental to the LHP. Now the obvious extremes are people whose sole source of self definition is their job, their race, their gender, their political party, their hobbies. You've met the type, the first thing out of their mouths is, "I am Object X." The feeling of revulsion from that sort of collective thinking was what lead most of us to striking out on the Left Hand Path in the first place. The beginning and most significant movements along the LHP always begin in solitude. But collectivism has a siren call. Some of us — probably all of us at some time — confuse the human organization called the Temple of Set with ourselves. This is another way of getting off the spot. We can either decide that we must be as good as Setian X, after all we own a medallion and Setian X owns a medallion — therefore we can through some practice of obscure osmosis absorb their charisma. Or the opposite approach can occur, we can stop using the mirror as our guide and decide to quit the Temple because Setian Y doesn't meet our criteria. Righteous indignation doesn't seem well dressed in a spiffy black wardrobe.

Concerning a Thought Experiment. The following visualization is offered as a thought experiment to interested people. Participation in this, as in any Setian ritual, is totally voluntary. Step one is here, step two will be in the post-Conclave *Scroll.*

• Visualize a hotel corridor. Behind all the doors on one side of the hall are a series of rooms special to you. As you open each room, you find that it magically opens to a place important to you from your past. Homes. schoolrooms, etc. Look around each. You may find that you have unresolved emotional or Initiatory items to deal with because of what you see. Being gentle and loving to yourself, try to deal with these in ways that benefit your Xeper. Remember that no matter where things were in your life, you can change it now— impelled by your Coming Into Being. You may find some long forgotten pleasures or interests. What do these tell you about your Self? You may wish to take them up again. See what step one does, and by your Will make what it does serve your Xeper.

Note Three

Concerning a Thought Experiment. Last *Scroll* I asked you to visualize the significant homes of your life as being on one side of a hotel corridor. Here's a question for you. What's on the other side of the wall, upstairs, downstairs, maintenance rooms, and so forth? What are the hidden areas supporting your Xeper?

Concerning the Festival of Khoiak. In ancient Egypt the season of Proyet, or Coming Forth, ran from November to February, and began with the Festival of Khoiak. The first job of that new season was a magical act of sowing grain on a field still muddy with receding floodwaters. A black ass, representing Set, was led through the field to trod the grain into the Earth so that they might grow. We Setians have trod many seeds into the Earth during our recent Conclave in San Francisco. We have lain the groundwork for new frontiers in Cyber-magic, we saw the first public working of the Order of Horus, heard the presentation of the Order of Kronos, were entranced by the Graal Rite Sir Loki created for an open Order of the Trapezoid Working, heard about new growth and reorganization in the British Isles, saw the Order of the Trapezoid's new Grandmaster at Work, saw the Order of Leviathan enthroning a new Grandmaster, heard a beautiful message from the Order of Amon, and we Cast our Vision of what we hoped the Temple shall be in the Is-To-Be. The number of folks who deserve thanks for the Conclave of this magnitude is very large, but special thanks go to Maga Aquino for her heroic efforts in bringing this off.

There were a plethora of goodies for sale including Adepts B's spellbinding paintings, the S's gargoyles, the L's engravings, Adept D's t-shirts, and much more. One of the cleaning staff was very impressed with the gargoyles, leaving them a money offering the first night they guarded our meeting room/ritual chamber. We had two live music performances, one from the Set Amentet Barber Shop Quartet, the other Adept U demonstrating the dijeridoo. We had dramatic readings, late night rituals, heard Enochian, German, Sanskrit, Egyptian, Yuggothic and the *voces magica* in various rituals. We heard wisdom and folly, learned discourses on Afro-Asiatic tongues, reflected on Heidegger, Aristotle, Kant, and Descartes. We saw card tricks and legerdemain, heard the music of Willie Nelson and the wedding hymn that Priest L had created for his marriage. We chanted, we danced, we drummed, we drew. We heard about Workings involving satellites soon to carry our Word beyond Saturn, and watched discoveries recently made by Magistra I on astronomical ceilings over three thousand years old. We discussed the role of the martial arts in the Left Hand Path and made some movement toward creating our own tradition. We saw new Houses Come Into being in the Order of the Trapezoid.

Concerning a Stela. I presented Dr. Aquino a Stela, designed by Magistra S and engraved by the Ls. It had the following inscribed on it:

For Michael A. Aquino,

A Stela

Composed on the First Day of the Egyptian New Year
as a Magical Link of the eternal Respect, Love and Blessings
that flow to him from the Dwellers in the Æon of Set
now and forever. 8/1/XXXI

I played my flute in the desert night,
and a special few heard the silvery call.
It was as subtle as the gem-hues of the Dark Light,
but it made for the Mind an everlasting Hall.

I gave what I had, which was the Way to the stars,
I gave it with tears and blood and sweat,
I gave it with Love, for with Love it had been made mine.
And they saw my magic treasure, saw it Dark and fine,
and heard it in their words, and drank it when they met,
and they grew wise on this earth, and shone among the stars.

I will not be remembered by all,
I didn't disturb the sands of time with Might,
but I will always be Remembered by those who Heard the Call,
when I played my flute in the desert night.

Note Four

Concerning this Year. This is the 22nd year of the Temple's manifestation. Twenty-two has a special place in Setian numerology. It is the number of the Bond with Set. This is expressed in a 22 word formula: Do What Thou Wilt Shall Be The Whole of The Law. Great Is The Might Of Set, Greater Still He Through Us. This is a quick guide for someone making an Initiatory decision. You have freedom to do anything that expresses your Self (true will) and of those actions, those which are most Set-like will speed your Xeper, accomplishing both your goal (personal empowerment on all levels) and Set's goal (exporting Xeper to the Objective Universe). This relationship, which creates the magical/social atmosphere of the Temple, is something to contemplate and act on during this year. You may wish to begin by comparing the above 22-word formula with this 22-word formula: "I Have Come Into Being, and by the Process of my Coming Into Being, the Process of Coming Into Being is Established." It is 93 years since the First Beast received his Word in Cairo.

Concerning the Four Paths. I was asked shortly before Conclave if I could "sum up" Setian Initiation. I sent a short summary to Xepera-L, where the question had been posed, and I spoke on it at Conclave. You may wish to keep this article, and discuss it with a Setian friend.

Setian Initiation may summed up in the alchemical formula *Solve et Coagula,* a Latin second person imperative: "You must dissolve and congeal." The processes involved are all going on all the time, but the bulk of the action is in the order presented below. The application of the formula is entirely individual. One thing to be noted about the formula is that most of the Work happens outside the Temple. Initiation is about life, the Temple is just a clue about Initiation.

Path of the West. (*Solve* without). I chose the attribution "West" for the Persian LHP metaphor of "going to the West" or "going to Egypt" as dealing with the world of Matter. The Initiate must begin by breaking her ties with the social matrix. They have to overcome the forces of conventionality and stupidity. The break with Church, State, Economy, Tradition, etc. is an act of rebellion. The breaking of social fetters both inside of and outside of the Initiate's head starts easy (we can all make fun of the Church or of a political party), and becomes hard (it's tough to undo a lot of early training). The Initiate even has to corrode some of that matrix in their lives by outrageous action. Some examples of success in this path would be running a "dark" occult bookstore, being a lawyer that takes on tough civil liberties cases, a career in rock-n-roll, doing front line work to separate Church and State, or leading a bike gang. You can probably think of a half a dozen more. All of the Work of the Church of Satan falls into the path of the West. It is the path of total Indulgence, that is to say, the path of Matter.

Path of the South. (*Solve* within). I chose the attribution "South" because the Egyptians saw the South as the place of Life. The word "to pray" in the Egyptian language means "to face the South." The Initiate turns to face the most important of all magical tools, his body. The way he deals with it must be broken down. Firstly he has to get rid of his destructive habits, then he has to train the body to be a vehicle for his will. He needs to know about sleep, nutrition, exercise, longevity training and so forth. He has to learn to use the body to Re-Create himself (this can vary from learning how to use nature to sex magic). He has to discover where his body came from by investigating the Becoming of his family. This includes *Magica Genetiva*, the study and practice of magical systems objectively linked to the operator by genetics or language. He must learn about his brain and body from the best scholarly resources he can handle (reading *Culture in Mind* isn't a bad start). Some examples of success with this path would be becoming a neurosurgeon, an anthropologist, running your own alternative medicine clinic, a teaching-level martial artist, a yogin, etc.

Path of the North. (*Coagula* Within). I chose the attribution "North" because of the Constellation of the Thigh. Setians generally face North when performing Greater Black Magic. Of this path which faces the Seven Stars, little can be said. The Initiate must come up with her own unique synthesis of the materials of her life. She has clues as to what this might be — firstly from the Sense of the Hidden that we call Rûna, secondly from those epiphanies of Self that we call Remanifestations. But the moment comes, and will come again and again in an Initiate's life — the true clarity of touching her potential. These moments of Self Crystallization always occur alone, and there is no recipe that can be given them. The Setian is always on the lookout for them, and values them above all else. Examples of success — you when you are at your best.

Path of the East. (*Coagula* without). I chose the attribution "East" because of the dawn. Xepera is the Dawn. Having transformed himself the Initiate now Needs to interact with people in a positive way. He needs to Teach his synthesis both within and beyond the Temple. This can be to his fellow employees at work, his children, his fellow Setians, the world at large. He is like the sun in the dawn, he makes people begin to see things that were Hidden to them. Some examples of success in this path would be employment as a teacher, a psychologist, a writer, trainer of any sort.

As you can see, these paths are lifetime paths. No one can claim success in all of these areas, which makes them perfect for Initiates. Initiates always seek out jobs that are too big for one lifetime. The Left Hand Path is hard, but it is never boring. The paths illustrate the basic principle that all of Temple experience is an illustrative Working for the rest of Life. Just as the Work in the Chamber is to a specific goal, so all Temple Work is to Life as a whole. If you're still struggling with the

"Are we Satanists?" question, try this — the standard position of the Setian is standing in the West, looking toward the North.

It's pretty easy to be egoistic on the LHP. We are after all sharper than 99 per cent of humanity. The possibility of what we can Become should however create some true humility. Balance these two, pride and humility, and you will find yourself empowered beyond your wildest dreams.

Note Five

Concerning our enemies. The Temple of Set is opposed by three powerful cults. These cults are pervasive, merciless, and untiring. They must be fought in all of their manifestations. Their names are the Cult of Stupidity, the Cult of Conventionality, and the Cult of the Victim. You should record each of your victories over them in your magical diary — your Victory Book. Your life should be a series of victories over these cults; do not be distracted and think minor cults like Christianity are our enemies. This is the Trinity we oppose:

The Cult of Stupidity teaches that it is a bad thing to be smart. The cult begins in secondary school where smart people are held not to be popular. It uses words like "nerds," "geeks," and even "brains" to exclude those individuals who concern themselves with the mysteries. It exists in the workplace where many topics are deemed "too deep" for discussion during coffee break, and a person is made to feel alienated if he were to talk about things like "why we are here."

The Cult of Conventionality teaches that there is an idealized form for your life to take. Usually a heterosexual monogamous marriage with 2.3 children with a home in the suburbs, a TV, and at most a dozen books in the house. This cult questions every decision you make from how you achieve transportation, to whom you sleep with (or refuse to sleep with), to your own reproduction. This cult in short claims to own your body.

The Cult of the Victim teaches that only by suffering are we redeemed. This evil cult takes over good movements of social empowerment by taking away the quest for power, and replacing it with a plea for justice for past social injuries. It allows people to engage in the worst behavior, and then be forgiven because of real or imagined illness or real or imagined abuse. This cult works against anyone with a big heart — and is particularity strong in cultivated circles. Beware of anyone who uses their bad situation as a path to power. Often they don't know better, this cult is so powerful.

There are forces that oppose these cults, these are our allies in battle, and deserve a helping hand from time to time.

These cults have made inroads into all discourse, even we may spout their pernicious slogans. Watch your speech and actions for signs of their influence. Do whatever yoga you need to train yourself out of them, this is where Crowley's techniques to avoid saying "I" and so forth are of the greatest good for the LHP practitioner. Work to remove these cults from your home and office — so that you won't keep having the same influences injected into your mind every day. Ending the practice of these cults is being faithful to Maat. Maat, sometimes translated as Justice but more correctly beauty, comes from *maa*, the verb "to see." The Setian must create and see justice around herself.

Concerning Occult Knowledge. "Occult" means "Hidden." That means that you won't find occult knowledge in mass-produced books. Real Hidden knowledge comes to the Ear, the Eye, or the Hand. I'll give you a very trivial example of the second. A movie theater that I frequent has a small overcrowded parking lot. It's a real pain to park there for a film, either you have to walk a long way to the movies, or sometimes you don't get a parking space at all. Now it so happens that the cinema is next to a large office complex, which has an underground parking lot. I wandered around there once during my daily walk. The underground lot has four spaces that are free to park in. The spaces are next to an elevator that opens less than 200 feet from the cinema, although not directly in view of it. Now I have occult knowledge. I park five minutes before the movie starts, I walk indoors less than 300 feet, and my car is protected from weather or vandals. Now like true occult knowledge, I would never let people in on it. If everyone knew — or even all my friends — those four slots would be taken up and I would lose my power. However, I can use this knowledge when I need to empower others — say someone that is taking me to the movies. Eventually the power will fade, so I must use it preciously. That is the nature of occult secrets.

The Setian must unlearn the RHP practice of telling everybody everything they know. It is hard to keep a Secret, keeping one is opposed to the Cult of Conventionality which wants to know and judge whatever one knows. It is likewise a sin against the Cult of Stupidity, which disapproves of effective knowledge in any form.

The Setian must learn when to speak and share, when to Teach and when to keep silent. He must also learn that real Secrets seldom look like the keys of the universe to the profane.

Concerning the Word. The Egyptian verb "Xeper" is cognate to the Hebrew word KLP (Keth, Lamed, Pe). For Cabalists out there this gives it a value of 118 (now you have a response when a Thelemite says "93" to you, and 25 points better — Xeper = Thelema plus *Yezech*, "to be separated"). The verb's meaning in Afro-Asiatic languages related to Egyptian offer some valuable clues to its meaning. In Hebrew, "to pass on, pass away, change, to come anew, to sprout;" in Syrian and Aramaic "to exchange"; in Arabic "he came after, succeeded" (this is the root of the word, "Caliph"). The Word entails movement — going from place A to place B, or something finishing, or something beginning again, or trading one thing for another. All of these speak of Xeper. We Xeper when we exchange a bad behavior for a good one, a bad partner for a good one, a bad home for a better one. We Xeper when we have traveled — an entire Order of the Temple is founded on this — the Quest aspect of Xeper. We Xeper when we cause a one-time good behavior to return, or when we take an activity to its next higher step — another Order is founded on this principle.

Note Six

Concerning the Dogma of the Temple of Set. I have heard it said recently that the Temple of Set has no dogma. That is incorrect. We do. Here it is. You may wish to write it down:

1. Being and Becoming are Good.
2. Being and Becoming can best be acquired by conscious, rationally-intuited means.
3. The Temple of Set, if properly used and maintained, is among the best Tools for acquiring Being and Becoming.

Concerning the custom of *Inw*. The Egyptian economy was neither a capitalist nor a communist economy. It ran on a system of gift-giving. The word for gift is *In*, plural *Inw*, as in *In Sutk* "The Gift of Set." *In* could either gifts from foreigners to the Pharaoh, gifts from the Pharaoh to his nobles, gifts to or from the gods, or gifts from the nobles to the people. Wealth and magical/religious power was circulated by gift giving. Things which were given became Holy, full of power.

In has two aspects in the current Temple of Set— one illustrative, the other operant. The illustrative component is found in the idea of the Black Flame, Set's **only** gift to us. There are many meditations for the Setian in the idea of the Black Flame. Why should such thing be given? What (if any) is the obligation in receiving the gift? Magus Flowers wrote one of the best essays on Set and his Gift for distribution at the Salem Conclave a few years ago. If you have not seen it before, I would like you to look it over and discuss it with your fellow Setians:

I. Set is the Principle of Isolate Intelligence.

II. It is dynamic (evolving).

III. Its purpose is self-maintenance, expansion, and perpetuation. This is its only good — otherwise it is beyond good and evil.

IV. It is not omnipotent — it must work for the changes it causes.

V. It is not omniscient — it must work to see objectively.

VI. Its Gift of Self is *perfect* (complete).

VII. It can *inform* or "teach" those possessed of its quality.

VIII. To give more (if possible) would be to *take*.

IX. The presence of the Gift in us (flesh) is *necessary* to the evolution of the Principle of Isolate Intelligence.

The operative aspect of *in* is Gift-giving between Setians. At the Dallas Conclave the custom of *in* was begun. Priestess X and I gathered a few cheap copies of several reading list books and set them out for interested Setians to take home. This was an interesting meditation. When you give a Gift, it is indeed gone. Sometimes things were picked and then dropped in the hotel lobby. Other books were the launching pad for various articles we've seen in the *Scroll* or of rituals we have heard about. Now this sort of Gift-giving is not appropriate for international gatherings where Customs officers might not be too understanding, but this sort of passing on — whether it's candle holders to Reading List books — is a formula that may wish to experiment with. You will learn more about the Gift, if you enact its dynamics.

If you are interested in *In* and its aspects both in the Egyptian economy and in Egyptian politics and religion you should read *The Official Gift in Ancient Egypt* by Edward Bleiberg (Univeristy of Oklahoma Press 1996).

Note Seven

Concerning the Munich Conclave. At Set-I in Windsor, Canada we began a Working Year of Conclaves to make the Temple of Set an international organization, and to proceed with our mission to export Xeper to the Objective Universe. At Set XVIII with the great and glorious help of Magister X and Adept U we have achieved this. The Workings and discussions about the Temple's future as we gear up for an even stronger level of manifestation were the best I have ever seen, and I must say the Order of Leviathan Working was among the most intense group Workings I have ever had the privilege to attend. The Order of Horus has its second Grand Master in the person of Magister H. The Order of Merlin performed a strong Working to lay the foundation of that Order, and certain magical Secrets were revealed at that time. The OV Working was particularly intense, and the I° and II° was very good from the reports I heard. Priest M's presentation on the reAwakening of the Uralic tradition was a rare moment to watch the opening of a Door that will change the North, from what it is to what it should be.

We all enjoyed the castle tours, and many of the Americans took the time to travel through Europe before or after Conclave. During the main Conclave Working, penned by Magister H, we ceremonially laid down the foundation for the Temple in Europe, a Recognition of the long and hard work of Magister X, Magister J and Priest M.

Things are really going to start cooking in the Old Country, now we turn our Attention to equally hard Work done 'round the Pacific Rim . . .

Concerning the Pergamon Working. In his best-selling book *Revelations* St. John the Divine said of Pergamon, that it was the "seat of Satan" where "the deep things of Satan were known." Turkey with cult centers like Tarsus was particularly known for its Left Hand Path pre-Christian Gnostic cults during St. John's time, but why did he pick Pergamon as **the** seat of Satan?

The answer is the Pergamon Altar.

Which on September 9, 1878 Carl Humann began digging for in Pergamon so he could ship it to Berlin. Berlin was on its way to becoming a world capital then (as now). Of the 14 buildings that constituted the acropolis of Pergamon (including a library second in size only to that of Alexandria) the great altar offers certain "problems" to archaeologists. Not in its magnificent style, nor in the transition it shows between Hellenic and Hellenistic thinking, but in the *relationship* between gods and men.

Berlin is perhaps the most energetic city in the world right now. For years it was a sort of odd-ball place, the German government used to pay subsidies to kooky people and artists to live there so it was a wild Bohemian place, but after the unification money came to Berlin. Big money. Lots of Money. Did I mention money? So the city is a forest of building cranes. The wasteland around that sorry-looking (and now hard to find) Wall is prime real estate. Twenty million tons of rubble have been carted out of the city in the last nine years. In the center of town there are perhaps 150 building cranes. Looking at a relief of Set and Sodpu in the Bode Museum, I thought how completely at home he looked.(All the neon in the East is powered by a single turbine connected to Joseph Stalin's grave . . .)

Pergamon was the great center of energy of its time. The Hellenistic kings of Pergamon decided to make their city — once a dependent Greek colony — into the base of an empire with Pergamon as a "new Athens." The Temple to Athena, which stood alongside the Great Altar, was the home of the great library. The rulers of Pergamon were known for their artistic self enhancement, and in addition to creating the art that became the ruling paradigm of the High Hellenistic age, they deliberately set about becoming the new cultural and scientific center of the Greek world. As Phillip von Zabern writes in *The Pergamon Altar*, Pergamon sought to be "the successor and legitimate heir of the fifth and fourth century Greek culture . . . In arts and this aim encouraged a revival of the golden age of classical Athens. Municipal authorities were elected in order to give the appearance of democracy even though municipal affairs were in actuality determined by five strategists hired by the king."

The rebuilding of the great altar in Berlin was a magico-political act of the new Germany. Contemporary admirers to its unveiling described Pergamon thusly: "an ambitious center of power and culture where one had the means to attract the finest craftsmen." The Seat of Satan built an empire in the popular German mind, and will now do so in the elite Setian mind, once its Secrets have penetrated. It was a magical Work in stone for King Eumenes II, for Bismarck, and now for us. We owe St. John a note of thanks for locating the Seat of Satan for us.

In the average Greek temple there is a central altar, easy to get to (after all, you're leading a steer behind you which you will slaughter and burn for the gods). The friezes showing the principal god are up high above you, so you know for certain that as the smoke of your sacrifice rises, it is surely reaching the noses of approving Olympians.

But not at Pergamon.

Here the central altar is on a raised platform. You have to climb 24 steps (from Alpha to Omega) to reach it. You are then standing **above** a frieze that shows the gods fighting the giants. The stairway you have just ascended had been worked into the composition of the lower frieze — gods and giants literally stand, kneel and lie on its steps. At the level of the altar is another frieze showing the life of Telephus, the mythical founder of Pergamon.

So I went and I looked and I Understood why St. John was terrified.

The life of a man, his struggles, his triumphs, his marriage to the Amazon Hiera, his kingship and founding of Pergamon are shown here.

Here are the "problems" of the altar. It is unclear what god or goddess the altar is sacred to — some guess Zeus, others Athena. It is very unclear how sacrifices would have been hauled up the steep steps, it has even been suggested that perhaps no burnt offerings took place here. Stranger still scholars are at a loss to say why the humans are at a higher level than the gods.

I went, I saw, I Understood.

Telephus represents the Mind of an Initiate. He is born of Herakles, he is abandoned at birth but fights his way to kingship. He is wounded and must quest to be healed by the very instrument that wounded him. He must do acts of evil and good to get what he needs. He creates empire.

His Becoming was on a higher plane of existence than the gods' battle with the giants. His struggle is the center. Temporal Becoming is exalted over the eternal struggle of the gods and giants. The gods are the idealized product of the minds of heroic men and women that are engaged in the good fight against the forces of naturalization — the five percent or so of society that progress when placed in stressful situations.

Telephus represents the even rarer breed whose actions produce in the world the stimulus for those touched of divine fire. Telephus, whose name by Greek *stoichia* reduces to 3, the Nous; is in short the model of a Setian. His relationship to the gods is our relationship to the gods. Our lives inspire them, from our struggles flows the energy to the elite of mankind that they in turn use in the ceaseless struggle against the forces of naturalization.

The only sacrifice that was offered at the central altar was the sacrifice of words — of saying what you plan to Do. The two messages out of Pergamon are firstly the relationship of our Xeper to the "gods" of mankind (in the fullness of time we are above, they are below), and secondly that Knowledge of that relationship is Power.

This may sound very simple, almost simplistic. Perhaps it is. There are a class of Secrets that don't take a genius to understand, but take a Genius, an Artist or a Hero to use.

Others had worked here. I think the reason that Gregor A. Gregorius had spent five years living in East Berlin after the war was so that he could work here. The altar had opened to the world in 1902, you may draw your own conclusions as to its effect on German occultism.

Thus it was and is the Seat of Satan from which all power flows into the world, and from that place on September 16, XXXII I ushered in the Millennium. I was assisted by Magistra I, Priestess X and Adept O. "Fate" had picked these beings to accompany me, just as it had picked them during my pilgrimage to Stonehenge where the Eternal Set Network was born.

The most easily seen results of this operation are threefold:

Firstly an ending of collectivist systems around the world. This has been in motion for awhile as one of the prerequisites for the coming of our Aeon. Berlin with its forest of building cranes is the best place in all the world to send this Idea into the world at this time.

Secondly a return to pre-Christian LHP sophistication in a post-Christian world.

Thirdly an increase in the abduction of the essential tools of other traditions into our own fold.

Of course, all of this is already going on, it was only from this stream of What Has Come Into Being, that such meaning could be found, ascribed and used. This type of magical use of altering emergent properties in accordance with the trans-temporal Will is the exclusive formula of the Aeon of Set.

Now will this all this happen auto-magically without tons of hard work on your part? Yes, of course it will — exactly as a jet takes off from the airport without your help. Of course if you're sitting on your couch at home when the jet flies away — you've missed your chance. If, on the other hand, you are paying attention to the flight schedule, and you have enough control of your life to take advantage of the flight, you can go anywhere.

At Pergamon, at the Seat of Satan, in the middle of the biggest construction site on the planet, I put out the Boarding Call. Some of you will think very carefully on this and make the flight— others will think that this is very cool, or just another article to fill up the pages of the *Scroll*.

We may send you postcards. If we are not too busy, or having too good a time.

Note Eight

Concerning Elements. The term "element" or "project" has been used in Temple literature for some years to describe certain experimental teams, whose function differs from that of a Pylon or an Order. Now this term has a very vague focus from: "We don't know what the hell this is, but it's a good thing" to: "This is a laboratory/factory producing a magical Substance that the Temple Needs." (Note this is not a physical substance but a metaphysical one, such as the substance called Vampyre). Both of these ideas are correct and accurate. Let's look at the terms in use and focus a little more clearly on "Elements."

Pylon. A gateway to the Temple of Set, named after the massive stone works of the XVIII and later dynasties when Mesopotamian architectural fashion became trendy in the Egyptian empire. Pylon gates were covered with victorious scenes of the empire, and had a narrow opening despite their huge structure. They dominated the landscape. Our idea of a Pylon derives from this military/magical image — which flourished during the height of Set's popularity as a war god. Pylons should be able to do five things. 1) Provide a safe haven for Initiates to learn the Arts of Black Magic by Doing. 2) Provide a surveillance of their area to both attract good things to the Temple and fight off the forces of naturalization. 3) Cause the Temple to be a unified philosophical entity by having its members of various Orders demonstrate their activities to each other. 4) Help new I°s explore the Temple by example and (if possible) face-to-face interaction. And 5) Provide a local or magical context for initiation that helps open interior gateways (this is usually done by interacting with the magical/historical heritage of the region). Ideally Pylons outlast their founder and Become permanent geographic gateways in the world. Of course such Work isn't the primary aim of the Pylon. We are not interested in more members, only better ones. However the Pylon — because of the members' hard Work on themselves — will attract other strong people willing to undertake the Work. Pylon Work is dangerous because it can become routine and therefore deflect the force of Xeper. It can deflect the force of Xeper by allowing the notion to slip in that doing rituals and having discussions are Initiation, rather then reminding us that initiation happens in the world; the Temple is merely a Tool to teach us about making the other Tools of Initiation.

Order. The Art of the Master of the Temple is the Art of War. She has found a set of practices, ideas, and images that have aided her development by keeping her Awake. Now to make these forces stronger in her, she takes the step of Speaking them to the Temple. She will grow from this testing of her ideas, preparing her to Do more in the worlds within and without. Her students are offered a chance to participate in the development of Work that is fresh, new and potent — as opposed to the weary magic that can be learned in the world from countless occult books. Orders may Become trans-personal as those who Learn become those who Teach. The Order of the Trapezoid and the Order of Leviathan have done this. Order Work is dangerous in that it can allow too many sentimental factors to slip in and we can lose the reason for our being here.

Element. Headed by a III°+, an Element (or Project) is a hands-on exploratory tool that will exist only as long as Needed. It will have a focus of experimentation and a certain knowledge that experimentation is dangerous. Now such a group would be bound by the ethical standards of the Temple of Set, and those that arise in the minds of mature adults. Elements will give themselves over to the exploration of various ideas and techniques, and their members will report to the Temple. Currently we have four such entities in the Temple. The Meta-Mind-Element headed by Magister O, which explores the uses and possibilities of extrasensory perception; the Arkte Warriors led by Maga Lilith Aquino, which explores the use of empathy with animals as a way of Self-development in a variety of forms from Amerindian shamanism to political activism; the Black Lotus, headed by Priest J, which explores the recreation of yoga as an LHP Tool. Element work is dangerous because it is not only going off in a new direction, but there will be times when blind alleys will suck precious time.

Now will we keep elements? Maybe. Some will produce the incandescent electric light — one of Edison's biggies – others may produce the electric stencil pen — not one of Edison's better moments. It will entirely rest on their track record.

Concerning Realpolitik. The Temple of Set as an organization has enemies. This is a good thing, because it helps us keep an edge to what we do. The fact that each of us has the potential in our Awakening to Become individual Temple of Set, means that each of us is faced with choices. We do not inherit any kind of "official enemies" list. But we also know that many of the people who have a similar aesthetic to ours, do have "official enemy lists." You should use enlightened self interest in dealing with these people. If you are dealing with folk that would like at some time to have you or your friends on the other side of a firing line, you have lost the first rule of LHP practice— self protection. If you enter a situation like this, no LHP endeavors will show up later. You will just get your fingers burned.

Now I don't break bread with people who hang out with folks that have made death threats on me, my family or friends. Like all Setians — the most important (and ultimately the only) gift I can others is the gift of my self — and for reasons magical as well as personal I choose not to have that force deflected.

Now, is this a suggestion that the Setian will shun the various LHP groups in the world? No. It suggests two things. 1) If you Play with scum you will become like them rather than Working the magic that will change them for the better. Read their publications and consider this —

the level they write at is the best thing they can imagine — it is the Limit of their Becoming. If that Limit is far below yours, you will only devolve in their presence. (Not to mention the fact that such Satanic wannabes are walking around with targets on their backs as their approach to dealing with the World of Horrors is further and further out of date.) 2) The Setian knows that the LHP is the training ground for Sovereignty— so he or she may wish to exercise his or her Sovereignty in occult circles. This is fine; although such efforts should always be seen as the most minor forms of power that one can find: If you are trying to lead kindergarteners your sense of victory will be getting them to put on coats before they go out in the rain, rather then seeing them becoming doctors and lawyers and bankers through which you rule the world.

One of the strongest forces of naturalization is the natural human tendency to rise or sink to the level of those around us. In order to fight that tendency, we must not only struggle with ourselves — watching out for our two worst foes: our secret intolerance and our desire to be liked — but we have to surround ourselves with people of quality. Now this is not the first commandment to earning a living, but it is part of the long-term Work.

Concerning the Left Hand Path. We are often confused about the nature of the Left Hand Path. The Right Hand Path is based on **Submission**. You only have one choice — where am I in my development to find what to submit to?

In the Left Hand Path you have the keyword **Moderation**. How much do I submit to the Path today?

In a RHP process you would have, for example, the option of "pure thoughts and chastity" say in Christianity or "orgies" say in Crowleyanity. We have to choose, and that opening ourselves up to Choice is how we discover our Secret governor. We might choose orgy today, pure thoughts tomorrow — or even go to the orgy and think pure thoughts.

The problems with Left Hand Path thinking is that many people assume that they are developed enough to make these choices, when in fact that have not yet begun to find and understand what their higher self is telling them. We each find that we are not developed to make our choices, and this should be a constant source of humility for us. But, I hear the agonized shriek, aren't we supposed to be Prideful of Being? Of course you are, but it is Pride that comes from seeing your sense of Daring at Work in the world. True magical Sovereignty comes not from thinking how great you are — but from Knowing that your sense of courage is greater than the rest of the world, so that you will win much more than the half-alive zombies next to you. The LHP alchemist takes the positive force of Pride (of Recognizing one's real accomplishments), the negative force of humility (of Recognizing one's limits), and the synthesizing force of the Black Flame and produces a Fourth Force — their empowered Selves.

If you remove some of the mix — let's say you take away the negative force of humility and the synthesizing force of the Black Flame — you get sociopaths. They find a place where they can be god — the Internet is best for this — and they practice such petty evils as give them minor thrills. Treating such individuals as though they have any meaning is reacting to a nonexistent force. Now **using** such creatures is all right and amusing — if you remember two things: 1) You're not really using a screwdriver, you're using a broken case knife. Throw it away when you're done and get something decent for your toolbox. 2) Even leeches expect to be paid.

Concerning Rûna. Picture if you will a tent in the desert night. It is a small tent, without much room for the person inside. She decides to make it larger. She raises the roof pole, and she adds fabric to the outside. A simple picture. Now think of this, as we become more godlike on this plane, we have to raise the roof pole — we have to increase our purely rational mental states. When we do this we have more room for Consciousness, real consciousness rather then the sleeplike state that most of humanity spends all their time in. We have more Freedom, real Freedom which is "Moderation" above. But each question we have answered has of course lead to ten more, so we have produced more Rûna in the world. Rûna is the covering of the tent, whose *surface area* increases — so that there is more Rûna in the Objective Universe, which is tern allows more people to awaken. So here's your job, my job everyone's job, is to increase our rationality, to give us more Freedom (Thelema), and more Awakened Consciousness (Xeper), while increasing the Mystery in the Objective Universe — which leads to more people finding Xeper. This job has come forth form behind the Constellation of the Thigh, manifest by the particular actions of many people in our Aeon, and its placement in the stream of world history when creation Freedoms can be gained by hard Work, and certain means and media of Casting Forth the Black Flame have appeared is no accident. This is time — through hard Work on ourselves —-that we are able to free ourselves from some of the hazard that is the lot of the race of man. Think on this, picture your tent, and talk with your Setian colleagues on ways to further the job in your lives.

UNCLE SETNAKT'S PICKS AND PANS

These are items too transient for the Reading List, which have caught my eye. By no means seek them down unless they tickle your magical fancy.

The Aryan Christ: The Secret Life of Carl Jung by Richard Noll- (Random House, 334 pg. $25.95 1997). Magister EO gave me this volume. (Thank you, E, I'm behind in writing my cards.) It is an analysis of the magical and organizational practices of Carl Jung. Although Noll is unsympathetic to Jung's magical practices such as his self deification, his use of occult materials, his messianic goals — he analyzes them well. One of the signs of a Magus' success is that his enemies — his intelligent thoughtful enemies — understand the ideas of the Work. The other interesting aspect of this work is an analysis of how Jung used the forces of the times (macro-politics) and the persons he met (micro-politics) to further his goals in the world. Now Jung is one of the most successful magicians of the twentieth century — far outdistancing guys like Crowley. If you are interested in Jung, this book is essential reading. If you are interested in using the forces of the world to further your ideas in the world, this is a book that shows what has Worked. Magister EO has wisely seen the connection between the Pergamon's influence on the German-speaking world and Jung, and offers this as a great "How-TO" book for changing the next Millennium.

The Struggle of the Magicians: Exploring the Teacher-Student Relationship by William Patrick Patterson (Aerte. 300 pgs, $16.95 1998). The real title of the book should be "Why Uspenskii left Gurdjieff." This book studies the relationship between Gurdjieff and his famous pupils Uspenskii, Orage, Toomer, Bennett, and so forth. It places their interactions in both a general and an occult historical context. It deals with Gurdjieff's concept of the Magus, and of the nature of Magic in the Work, which is defined as capturing someone's attention, clarifying it, and then directing it. The book deals a great deal with the concept of *Mêtis* (Μητις) which Gurdjieff describes as the primary virtue of the (LHP) Sovereign. *Mêtis*, usually translated as "cunning" in English, is a type of knowing and thought formed by a complex but coherent "body of mental attitudes and intellectual behavior which combine flair, wisdom, forethought, subtlety of mind, deception, resourcefulness, vigilance, opportunism, various skills and experience acquired over the years. It is applied to situations which are transient, shifting, disconcerting and ambiguous, situations that do not lend themselves to precise measurement, exact calculation and rigorous logic." The book deals with the struggle of the Teacher-Student relationship, as well as with Gurdjieff's methods of stopping automism in people. The author is an absolute follower of Gurdjieff, and some of the hero-worship is a bit thick, but the observations on the power, nature and scope of the Work speak well for the volume.

Note Nine

Concerning the Year. This is the 33rd Year of the Emerald Dawn, a time of great Freedom for those that take great Responsibility. I Declare this to be the Year of Cthulhu Rising, this being the 70th anniversary of the publication of Lovecraft's famous novella, "The Call of Cthulhu" in *Weird Tales* February 1928, which will see the Aeon of Set (so well established in the Pacific Rim by the Strivings of Priestess S and her heroic crew) take deep roots preparing for the next Millennium. This would be a good year for serious research into the mythology and archaeology of the Pacific, a good year for shaking off some Eurocentric thinking, a great year to be surprised by the Orders most connected with Cthulhu (i.e., the OL and the OTR), a nifty year to play with Nessie and other lake monsters, a wonderful year to explore the place of dreams in Initiation and Magic, and a cool year to have some fun creating fiction in the Setian Mythos project, and join in the examinations of the subconscious and art in the Order of Uart. Above all it will be a year to frequently engage in that important Black Magical meditation of just how BIG and BUSY the world is, and how if one keeps aware of one's Purpose that Awareness this makes the BIGNESS and the BUSINESS of the world into a constant source of advantage.

This will be a year of sending Dreams.

As I have written elsewhere, I was once given a great magical formula for dealing with the world by Magus S. Edred Flowers. Awaken, See, Act. The first part of the formula *Awaken* assumes two things. One that I have fallen asleep (and need to refocus my mind/body/soul), two that since the Subjective Universe has no location in time and space — any moment and any place can be a launching pad both to and from it. *See* assumes that I don't really know what is going on, and that surface appearances are misleading (i.e., the smiling man from the insurance company isn't really interested in my well being). The third term *Act* means that I must, in my quest for Sovereignty, Do something. The Left Hand Path is active, not contemplative.

Now where do Dreams come up in this most useful of formulas? Dreams are **Seeing** without being Awake. They are things taken in that the Mind can witness but not yet process.

Sending Dreams, which as magical texts show is one of the oldest of Setian arts, means Metacommunication.

Metacommunication includes any sending of message that is more than what it seems. This includes this essay, Art, Initiatory dialogue, Illustrative Magic and (what is sadly called) "Lesser" Black Magic. Because of the word "lesser" there is far too little attention paid to this most powerful of art forms. I am asking my Setian colleagues to spend a year thinking about, talking about, writing about, and practicing LBM. Like Cthulhu, the High Priest of the Old Ones, I expect you to become wondrously effective at sending Dreams.

Concerning Lesser Black Magic. We practice LBM for four reasons. First, to achieve goals that normal channels of communication won't allow us. Second, to enchant our lives. Third, to learn to lessen the effect of LBM upon us. Fourth, to produce internal friction and Awareness of Purpose. Let's look at each of these and then at the dangers of LBM.

To achieve goals that normal chances of communication won't allow us. As Magicians we strive to change the world around us to allow for more Freedom and more Opportunity. That is to say we are always trying to increase the likelihood and effectiveness of our Xeper. The way of the world does not support Freedom and Opportunity. The way of the world is to insist on its rules.

To enchant our lives. We practice LBM for fun. We may practice it by telling a ghost story around a campfire, a tall tale to a fellow airline passenger, or tell a sick friend that the tea you are giving them has magical powers that will make them feel better, or even giving that special someone a fortune cookie whose fortune happens to read, "Will you marry me?"

To lessen the effects of LBM on us. The world has a constant barrage of signals coming our way. A very small percentage is challenged by our consciousness. The rest just pours in. How many of you have tried to clear your mind and found that there was a Pepsi Cola advertisement running there? We will always be amateurs at LBM compared to Madison Avenue, but we will be armed amateurs.

To produce internal friction and Awareness of Purpose. The single greatest weakness of the Black Magician is egotism. Usually it is in the form of a semiautonomous part of the psyche that justifies all past action. In LBM situations where you have to learn not to talk all the time, not to let everyone know your every little thought, and spend more time listening than broadcasting, you learn your big purpose comes first. The person who knows she must rent the house for X dollars can screen out the chatter of the real estate agent — and by acting rather then reacting get her Wish, as well as get training of the Will. The practice of LBM creates the same temporal displacement of consciousness that enabled out ancestors' ancestors to Receive the Gift of Set as hunter/gatherers.

The danger in LBM is that is seductive. It can allow us to get out of a hard situation where we might Learn something into an easy situation where we will not, it can allow us to cheapen a relationship based on Truth into one based on manipulation, it can begin to tarnish the way we look at our fellow humans. Because of this a strong ethical background is needed. That is why you received the stand-alone essay on Setian ethics. Please read it, discuss it and write about it this entire year.

All seductive behaviors are seductive because they represent a regression to an earlier state. The natural mind confronted with stress reverts, the Setian Mind accepts this natural falling backward as time for regrouping, and waiting for a solution.

Remember that Setians choose to put themselves in hard situations so that they may Learn. Now many times they may only learn, that is to say, figure out a good rational plan. Well this is good because it teaches Reason, and Reason is always the best tool for acquiring Power in the world. But sometimes the thought situation may to lead of a moment of Xeper, that moment of Subjective realization of a Win:Win:Win solution, which is the test of Xeper a solution for the present, the future and eternity. But such things are rare — even when we put ourselves into various kinds of strife so that we have to come up with them.

Lesser Black Magic involves putting aside an existing set of rules for one of your own creation. It is therefore the Slaying of Osiris, who personifies rule systems. Lesser Black Magic is of four varieties: **Expansive**, **Constrictive**, **Penetrating**, and **Encasing**. Let's look at each of these four flavors:

Expansive Lesser Black Magic (or Werewolf mode) is breaking the rules by flaunting them outrageously. An example would be someone who discovers that they can go to any party they want in Yuletide by dressing up like Santa Claus. They can kiss anyone they want, scarf up any food they wish, get to talk with anyone. Expansive LBM is flashy and dangerous because as soon as you come across a person that's Awake, they aren't going to let you get away with it. Most rock musicians are in a permanent expansive LBM Working.

Constrictive LBM (Or Vampyre mode) is drawing another into your set of rules. An obvious form might be being very seductive to a waitperson in a busy restaurant to get better service. It involves enticing others to Play with you. It requires a great deal of knowledge of personal strengths and weaknesses, cunning patience and magnetism.

Constrictive LBM is dangerous because you run the risk of someone becoming too taken with you, and hurting them or yourself. Most movie starlets are in a permanent constrictive LBM Working.

Penetrating LBM (or Wizard mode) is having (or pretending to have) secret knowledge of the rules beyond the rules. For example it could mean parking your car in a No Parking Area when you know that rule isn't enforced between six and ten in the evening. Or it could mean getting a bumper-sticker that reads "Authorized Vehicle" and parking under a sign that says, "Authorized vehicles only." This mode requires curiosity, open ears and not talking about everything you know.

Penetrating LBM is dangerous because it can lead you to spending all your time learning trivial facts rather Learning life lessons. Most spies are in a permanent penetrating LBM Working.

Encasing LBM (or Bumpkin mode) is adding a rule or two to an existing set. For example let's say you are a grocer with too many cans of red kidney beans. So you put up a sign, "Red Kidney Beans — Limit One Can Per Customer" — and your customers fearing the red kidney bean shortage, will clean you out. Encasing LBM is dangerous because it is so easy to work, it can lull you to sleep and think that the rule is "real." Most midlevel managers are in a permanent encasing LBM Working.

How many times have one of these Workings been used on you?

Concerning the Material Question. We are living in an age of greater economic stratification, so it behooves the Magician to see to his or her wealth acquisition. The acquisition of wealth is not a goal in itself, and should never take a front seat to Initiation, but should be viewed as one of the easiest Keys to Freedom and Opportunity. Being Aware of the magnificence of existence is always more valuable to the Black Magician than mere pragmatic materialism, but pragmatic materialism is like Reason, a tool that the Black Magicians never puts away. The acquisition of wealth need not be money, but it should be the same sort of power. For example if you work for an airline that gives you free tickets, that is the power of gold. The Black Magician never neglects the world of matter, whether that means building up money, or taking care of the body. Matter is the best tool we've got. Now some of you may see some similarity in my interest in matter and that of the late Howard Stanton Levey. Levey wanted people to make money and send it to him, I say make money and keep it. If you are unclear on the difference between the ideas, send me a dollar by mail.

Concerning Schools and Jars. The Temple of Set is a School. It is not a jar. It is not a limited group to which and from which all Attention must be paid. One of the limiting fetters of minority groups is a tendency to view only members of the group as real. The Magician uses and Learns from all of mankind. If you want to start a group to study dreams (or whatever), you don't have to limit it to Setians. Go start one in your town. Now I wouldn't advise you walking in with your medallion on, nor for that matter with the words "DEVIL WORSHIPER" tattooed on your forehead. Do your Work, Learn what you want to learn (and learn something about human psychology, leadership and magic in the process), then Share your results with your Setian colleagues. Your job is to transform the world around you into a maximal Learning environment. The Temple is not a conduit to Power or even to Connection with your Self-Created nature — the Temple merely gives you a chance to learn methodologies that you must use to gain these things. Your magical life began long before you entered the Temple, and must extend far beyond it. Don't let the Tool become a totem, nor the School a jar!

Note Ten

Concerning Lesser Black Magic. Here is the most powerful formula for LBM: warn your mark of your intentions. If you are trying to make them buy a house by being nice to them, say, "Now some people might try to influence you into buying as house by being friendly to you." If they ask if you are doing this, admit that you could be, that they have to be the judge. This works every time. How many times has it been used on you?

Here's a second tip. Look for LBM Training seminars. The best are free seminars selling a product, that you can't afford and don't want. You get an ad in the mail saying that they have a valuable mock emerald pin they will give you if you come to their spiel for a house on Lake Mosquito. Go listen to the spiel, see how the crowd is moved, and experience the tough moment of breaking from the herd by saying, "No!" The Temple assumes no responsibility for those of you who lack the strength to say "No!" to a Realtor.

Notes toward a Cosmic Ecology. One of the Secrets of the Left Hand Path, realized in the Temple at the Second Degree, is that meaning is imposed by the individual onto a meaningless world. We have a model of the universe, hopefully up-datable, that determines what we see and how we act. Clearing this Cosmology of useless or contradictory notions is the ongoing task of every Initiate.

We all need a model of how humans act. I am going to suggest a model. It is only a model, not reality.

In the Papyrus Bremner-Rhind the Xepera Xeper Xeperu formula divided mankind into five races. These are not "races" in the sense that word is used in this world, but types of spirit determined by the divine ancestor one has. This division, which would be an examination of which Ka rules their actions, is a useful one in learning how to read people, and is particularly useful to people who derive their Power from the Xepera Xeper Xeperu formula. I will leave it as an exercise for you to see the LBM applications, as well as what benefits may come from using this model. But keep in mind one thing. We would all have some of each of these essences in ourselves, so this likewise explains certain sorts of contending ideas we may have, and can help us satisfy those needs so that we may proceed with our greater goals. The Five Races of Mankind are the Children of the Children of Earth and Sky. They are:

The Children of Osiris. Their approach to existence is that existence is best maintained by preserving what has gone before. Their rituals and slogans are based on preserving whatever they **have come to believe** is the past. They are the most numerous race, and provide a matrix for civilization to continue. They idolize the laws of nature as a guide for the laws of man.

The Children of Horus. Their approach to existence is to find their place in the hierarchy. Existence is a war against nonexistence, and everyone has a part and must find it. Their rituals and slogans revolve around self-knowledge and duty, and their test is social functionality. When they rally around an idea for change, such as the American Revolution, it takes off and becomes the new Order. They idolize the principle of mankind against the Cosmos as the guide for the laws of man.

The Children of Set. Their approach to existence is to pit themselves against limits (either social or personal). Existence is the feeling of resistance being overcome. Their rituals and slogans revolve around identifying and overcoming challenges. They idolize the principle of opposition as the guide for the laws of man.

The Children of Isis. Their approach to existence is self-sacrifice for the future. Maybe they didn't have it good, but their children (literal or figurative) will. Their rituals and slogans emphasize children. They idolize the potential of another's Becoming as the guide for the laws of man.

The Children of Nepthys. Their approach to existence is opting out of the world and living in a willed construct. The world they live in may be strong enough to change ours, or they may wind up as nutcases. Their rituals and slogans are idiosyncratic since you must enter into their worlds to understand them. Examples include the Emperor Norton, Salvador Dali, or H. P. Lovecraft. They idolize human creativity as the guide for the laws of man.

It must be stressed that these groups include non-initiates as well as initiates. A Child of Set might the angry guy that throws rocks at cars, a Child of Osiris might be the most brilliant scholar you know.

Before you pick up and use this pretty thing, there are some questions you should ask yourself:

Is this model useful for you? What would be the test for such a model? How do you deal with each of these parts of yourself? Who are examples of each of these groups? What is their place in the world community? In world history? In your life? What are the limits and dangers in such a model? You may also wish to try these questions on models you are already using.

Note Eleven

Concerning Houston. The Easter Weekend saw the Houston Conclave, a new high water mark in regional Conclaves. Preceded by the third annual gathering of the Order of the Trapezoid, the event saw many wonders. The Knights of the Order have a new King in the person of Magistra I, her name being forwarded for her confirmation as is their custom. There were discussions, magic, visits to such sights as the butterfly Garden, the Funerary Museum, and Leo's, which is the best Tex-Mex food in the world. Priestess Watson did a great job, and Priest X and all the good folk of the Black Phoenix gave great aid in producing this gem to be placed on the altar of Set. I was very moved since I had begun my journey into the Left Hand Path in Houston some nineteen years before, and the Temple took a great magical step forward by Awakening its egregore using certain technologies of the Fraternitas Saturni. Those of you who may wish to interact with this Work, should seek out one of the 40 or so people that were there for a certain sonic mystery. The egregore has four functions. Firstly, it draws to us new members of strength. Secondly, it causes our enemies to reveal their perfidy to us. Thirdly, it can give a boost of informing energy to newer Initiates. Fourthly, it gives a place for more developed Initiates to store some of their power. Of course, any such Working only works if the man and women involved feed it with resonant action.

Concerning the Layers of the World. Like most people involved in an Afro-asiatic magical tradition (in my case Setianism), I divide the world into four layers. There are as follows:

1. The surface level is the activities in the here-and-now. The changes wrought here are the most important to the development of the Self on Earth, yet for the most part they are of no consequence. A wrong turn of the wheel of your car may end your life, but deciding whether to have a cup of coffee is not likely to have that much impact in ten years. The magician has one way of effecting this level of activity. It is the formula of Awaken, See, Act. The surface level of being provides Freedom.

2. The medial level is the area most subject to programming. It is the part of the self where goals, dreams, habits, and desires lay. The human being is constantly full of notions, usually unexamined about what he or she would like to do and "should" do. Sometimes these notions are in conflict, often they are based on delusion. This area has to be cleared of unwanted programming, and filled with wanted programming. This part of the self is most easily effected by two forces: Self-Knowledge and Magic. Knowledge is an understanding of happiness and limits. Happiness is a self-determined and self-perceived state. Not only is what makes me happy not what makes you happy, it is very likely that you have seldom known true happiness, because you do not know your character. True happiness is not mere gratification, it is that which engages the greatest parts of your being. It is not the result of

Indulgence, which is the state granted by those things with which we can temporarily gain union; it is the state of knowing who you are by what has made you happy. Knowledge is based on a true understanding of limits of self. You won't be playing for the NBA if you are five foot two. You won't be Miss America if you're missing your two front teeth. Knowing your limits, knowing exactly what you are and then using your assets and overcoming your shortcomings, is the key to happiness. Magic is the art of changing one's medial activity so that certain results may be obtained in the inner and outer worlds. Magic can be useful in breaking bad habits, obtaining new perceptions, obtaining new resources and opportunities in the world; but its main use is in changing Perception. Magic allows you to see the world more and more from the point of view of a constant to which all else becomes a variable. This part of our existence is seldom perceived since our attention is usually within it. Unchecked, it is a place of worry and despair or idle daydreaming. When all of our attention is lost in the medial level, things feel unreal to us, or our friends tell us (quite correctly) that we are in denial. When we have balanced the medial level of ourselves, the symbols of our dreams are coherent. The medial level of activity can be directly observed as the "near death experience." Many people, myself among them, have had the interesting feature of their "life passing before their eyes" in a near-death experience. This rapid, deep, and surprising experience shows the value many events have had on shaping you. It clarifies many things. It also shows things that not only you would rather forget, but that indeed you had forgotten. Most people confronted by this kind of death experience will suffer at having done so little. "Gee, you mean at any time I could have done something about my wretched little life? Why didn't someone tell me?" The medial level of being provides Context.

3. The core level of dynamism is the unchangeable part of the Self. It exists as an absolute pattern for potential. In many myths, the core part of ourselves is the first land, the magical island rising from the watery depths. Here is that part of you which is unique, indestructible, and not directly observable— but its presence in the Cosmos sets up those situations that cause you to become aware firstly of your own existence, and then to sense what sorts of experiences might help with your development. It is, in short, the reason for your unique existence, all furthering of its development is the Work of the Left Hand Path. It is rarely perceived in our lives since our attention is loosely housed there. The core level of being is not static since it contains the principle of dynamism. The name for this core level is the Principle of Isolate Intelligence. The Symbol for the core level being is the Inverse Pentagram surrounded by (but not touching) a circle. The core level of being provides Individuality.

4. The daemonic level of activity is that experience that associated you with what are vaguely called "magical currents." This part of ourselves, which is as unified and semi-sleeping as the others, is the part

of ourselves that acts upon the Cosmos, and is acted upon by entities in the Cosmos on a magical level. It has access to data that is not bound in chronological time, it can cause effect at a distance, it can lead you to items and persons that are desirable even if you do not recognize their qualities due to their surface manifestations. It can even be seen under certain circumstances. This level of being may be partially inherited such as the Germanic *fylgja* or the Celtic banshee, or it may be invoked like the Holy Guardian Angel. The daemonic level of being provides Magic.

Each of these parts must be awakened, its sub-components harmonized, its place in the personal ecology controlled and regulated. Each of these parts is fed by and feeds the other parts.

The Cosmos has exactly the same four levels. By changing the four levels of yourself, the Microcosm, the Cosmos may be effected by Resonance. By studying the four levels of yourself, you may learn about the four levels of the Cosmos, and by studying the levels of the Cosmos you may learn about yourself.

1. The **surface level**. Here the Cosmos is very small: it is only that section that is interacting with you at a given moment. Even so, it is larger than you, and will remain largely hidden in the ways it is effecting you. A guideline for understanding this level of the Cosmos, is that it is the exercise equipment, you are the gym customer. There is nothing that is coming your way in a given moment that you are not strong enough to handle. The surface level provides Energy (and magic) from ancestral intent, which may seem like "bad news" but is often the "bad event that brings the Good."

2. The **medial level**. This is the sum total of all the subjective overlays that determine human events. This means what some occultists call the "World Soul," historians are apt are to call the "zeitgeist," and what futurists call "trends." The medial level is composed of historical forces, semiconscious remnants of thought systems, advertising, and herd prejudices. The forces in this heady mix are always in conflict. All of these forces act to take the place of thinking in individual human beings by a form of hypnosis. If the magician can learn to avoid the "spell" these forces place upon him or her, they are then free to use these forces. The magician realizes that these forces are Neutral in his or her struggle — that means that at any given moment about half of the forces are against you, and half on your side. The medial level of the Cosmos provides the magician with his or her unawakened Allies for various political, artistic, and social endeavors.

3. The **core level**. The Left Hand Path posits that its patron, the Prince of Darkness, the ultimate maker of patterns and potentialities, is the core level of the Cosmos. The Prince of Darkness chooses to be a finite being, so that It may enjoy its individuality. Unlike the all-powerful, all-encompassing being that the Right Hand Path would envision as God, the Prince of Darkness chose on a Cosmic level what those who would grow like him choose on a human level — the principle of Self-

development. The core level of the Cosmos provides the Model of divine individuality and independence. The Symbol for the Prince of Darkness is culturally determined. In a society ruled by Right Hand Path paradigms, the Prince of Darkness is the rebel against cosmic injustice, Satan. In a society where the release of energy from dissipating patterns is revered yet feared, it is Shiva. In a society that stresses the role of the LHP magician as culture hero, it will be the supreme god of the pantheon like Odhinn or Tezcatlipoca. In a society where there is no central paradigm but many competing at the same time, it will be Set, the god against the gods.

4. The **daemonic level**. This is the sum total of all magical activity on the world. The spells and enchantments that have Shaped the world are still active in it. Some are fairly obvious: The interactions of Dr. John Dee with Elizabeth I are why English is the primary language in the United Sates and Canada. Others are a tad more obscure, such the hippie culture's roots in Aleister Crowley's introducing Huxley to mescaline. Some may be of very small scale, such as a haunting, or as vast and mysterious as megaliths. These forces tend to prey on most would-be magicians causing them to "bow down" to the achievements of a past they are not wise enough to understand, but for those who see such things as triumphs of the human spirit, and use them as spurs to their own greatness, these magics of the past provide aid both as inspiration and amplification. The Left Hand Path initiate studies manifestations in the following manner.

1. Research in current scholarly resources on matters of interest. The Left Hand Path magician avoids the occultnik dreck that reflects another's poor understanding.

2. Personal synthesis on what is discovered based on our personal sense of Beauty.

3. Enactment of that synthesis.

4. Sharing the results of part three with those who are part of his or her School.

Each of these four levels (both microcosmically and macrocosmically must be engaged with by the Left Hand Path practitioner. Some will find certain levels easy to tap into, others difficult. Since the Left Hand Path is centered on the self, there is always the temptation not to enter into exchange with these levels, to be some sort of vampire that merely tries to absorb without giving. Such pathetic creatures may obtain a certain level of power in this world, but they remain small and twisted, they can not partake of the fullness of being that fair exchange allows. To work with the surface, you must dedicate yourself to those causes in the world that increase human freedom and potential. To work with the medial level, you must engage yourself in creation of such medial artifacts that increase human awareness. To work with the core level, you must lead a life that serves as a model of self-development. To work with the daemonic level, you must share the results of your research and experiments with others who are striving in the direction of the mysteries.

These eight levels of being, four internal and four external, are joined together by the act of Perception. This process requires not merely "looking" at things, but preparing yourself to see them — which may mean education, or getting rid of emotional baggage, or learning occult techniques. Perception beckons energy from the outer realms, and directs it into the inner realms. It is the source of nourishment, and as it improves by practice and the removal of delusion, it becomes the basis for unifying the Self in such a manner that coherent afterlife states are possible.

Concerning Lesser Black Magic. At the Houston Conclave, Adept O. uttered the greatest Secret about LBM, "You can get anything done in the world that you want as long as you don't care who gets the credit." If you can get your boss, your graduate adviser, your editor to think that it is really his or her idea, you can do anything. This is the LBM form of Odhinn's formula of "sacrificing self to self." Give up ego for Power. Works every time.

There will be times in your life when you are taken in by somebody's malicious LBM. The reaction you will naturally feel is not one of rage, but (oddly) one of guilt or inferiority. "I was stupid, I should have seen it coming" or "Well it was as much my fault as his. He didn't hold a gun to my head." This makes you carry bad things in your head for years after the perpetrator got off scot-free. Here is the Setian approach. First check to see if it is too late to do anything about the problem; your emotions can wait. Second, raise a toast to the person who got you, "Damn he/she was good. They outsmarted me!" (This is to short circuit guilt and inferiority feelings.) This is an antinomian action —it goes against the grain and will free up some power in your psyche. Three, write down an account of what was done to you in your magical diary. This is for two reasons. First it lets you find out **why** such things work on you, that is to say it contributes to Self Knowledge, which is ultimately empowering. Second you can use their methods — although hopefully in a more ethical fashion than they did. This is part of the standard Setian alchemy of turning any experience into gold.

Concerning the Temple-wide Working of 6/21/XXXIII. To celebrate the Night of Founding, we will have a simple, but powerful Working to explore the idea of resonance. Accurate magical work Resonates with Work done in the past — this is how a Setian living in Johannesburg in XXXIII has connection with Work done in Santa Barbara in X. And how some Setian living in Moscow in LX has some connection with the Setian in Jo-berg now. Creating such loops with reality is our part of our bargain with Set, it is his way of creating effective talismans in four-dimensional space.

The Temple-wide Working requires much planning and forethought. You will need to mark your calendars now. Here is the Working. It is in four parts. Part one. Pick seven things you intend to do for your Xeper. At least one must be inside the Temple (like writing an article for your Order's newsletter), at least one must be outside the Temple (losing five pounds). Some may choose tasks that they have long been planning to do, to fulfill an existing magical Oath; others will want to choose wholly new ones. Part two. On the day of North Solstice, at any time of your choosing, say the word "Set" — say it clearly and distinctly. You pick the place, the time, the volume, and so forth. Be creative. Why do you want to say the word at work, or on a ham radio? Why do you say it at home just before bed, or scream at the top of a mountain at one minute past midnight? Part three. Do each thing on your list. If you can't do one, pick a substitute. When you are sure that have finished the task (the article is printed in the newsletter, the scales show the five pounds are gone), say "Xeper." Say it clearly and distinctly. Now this makes you pick tasks that are discreetly doable — like reading a particular book rather than "I am going to work on my Spanish." The scope and variety of tasks are up to you. Some might be very simple like "I'll pay my dues on 6/21-and mail it that day!, others might be very tough "I'll climb Mt. Kilimanjaro." It makes you pick tasks that you can really do in a reasonable space of time, you really don't want this Working to last for years, because by then so many others will have taken place. It makes you tie the tasks back to the magical utterance you made in Honor of the Night of our Founding. Fourth part. This (oddly enough) is the tough part. Until you have finished your seventh task, and said "Set" the seventh time, **don't talk about your tasks**. Some of you may finish all the tasks the day of the Working, some may pick tasks that will last a lifetime. You are in competition with your fellow Setians. (Now don't panic if you screw-up and speak of a task too early, just calmly catch yourself and don't do it again.) However after you have finished your tasks, you should certainly meditate on what the Working meant for and did for you. Some of you may wish to share this Working with your Pylon, or the *Scroll*, or just with a close Setian friend. If someone wants to talk with you about their tasks, Listen carefully because you may Hear more than you think. Then just tell them that you are still on your Mission, and aren't ready to report on it. The last part of this job is to watch how over the next few months that follow, these tasks fit together. Sometimes you'll see simple connections, the Priest that decides he'll take his Pylon on a road-trip to some standing stones, might be pleased by the Adept who has decided to fix her Pylon a meal for Set's Birthday (July 29) volunteered to bring the food and do the little ritual out of *The Seven Faces of Darkness*, when they can both talk about their Work a few months later. Some of the connections will be a great deal more mysterious.

This is Setian magic at its best — focused on results in the Objective Universe, individually chosen and performed, yet esoterically tied to the Temple's job of exporting Xeper to the Objective Universe.

Note Twelve

Concerning Xeper. The eternal Word of Set, "Xeper," an Egyptian verb meaning, "I Have Come Into Being" is at the depth of all truly human experience; however the deep knowledge that we are responsible for our own creation is too great a strain on most of mankind. Although we draw from the core of all human action, we are not for all humans.

Xeper is the *Becoming* of *Being*. Life is possibility. There are different models of human experience. One would tell us that we are Being — some set of permanent ideals that merely need to be expressed by finding our true Wills (and adding the letter "k" to magic). Others would tell us that we are Nothingness — that all of the parts of ourselves exist only at this moment — and that an inspired craziness would be the Good. In the Temple of Set, we choose a path between those extremes. We are interested in the Becoming of Being. We believe that there are parts of us that are fixed and stable, but largely hidden from our direct perception except at those moments of extreme clarity, when we can Truly say "I Have Come Into Being!" But we also believe that Being can be acquired — from the rationally intuited and inspired use of the seemingly accidental parts of our lives.

This gives each of us not only the possibility, but the responsibility for Creating our own Worlds.

The Process by which Xeper can be discovered (= "uttered") by each human is unique to each human. The summation of that Process is found in the eleven word formula, "The target must not be perfect, but the method must be." Any magical process is aimed at imperfect targets. You are sick, so you aim a spell at your body. You have a bad job so you aim a spell at your employment possibilities. You do not aim a spell at a perfect target – you don't find a ten dollar bill in the street and do a ritual on it to make it an eleven dollar bill. The lifelong magical work of changing yourself obviously begins with an imperfect self. (That part is pretty easy for humans to come by, I believe that there are over six billion imperfect selves to work with right now.) The method, however must be perfect. It is not a simple matter of knowing your wants and abilities — what if you had had the chance to design your life when you were nine years old — you be pretty damn miserable right now— even if you did own all the Hot Wheels ever made. So the goal you are aiming for is both partially Hidden within you and changes as you acquire more being. The method then is: Choose your goals derived from your experience of Xeper — not from my words, or some book, or some guru you have met. Your goals will change, because they are only approximations of your Xeper, but the method of picking them relies on your only true guide, your own experience consulted in times of great clarity.

Xeper is the Eternal Word of Set, by which he accomplishes his goals in this and other worlds of Becoming. Set, a god alternately revered and loathed in ancient Egypt, is the god of separation from the Cosmos. His name in Egyptian means "isolator" or "elector." The "satanic pride" that we do engage in the Temple is by becoming Set-like. We do not worship this entity, but use him as a role model. Now most religions would teach that we are part of the universe, the Setian rejects this, and accepts the responsibility for his own success and failures — just as Set his spiritual father does on a divine scale. If an acorn falls from a great oak, it contains all the necessary potentials to be a great oak. But the acorn's job isn't to rot so that it can be absorbed by the root system of the oak. It doesn't seek unity. Instead it seeks to become another oak, which in its own time will make its own acorns. Love does not consist in my being one with the soul of my Lover, but contemplating all the things that make her special and unique from me and from the rest of the Cosmos. If I were at one with her, the amount of Love in our private world would be halved. With each new soul that claims for itself the heritage of the Prince of Darkness, the amount of Love, Mystery, Intelligence, Magic, Play, Music, Memory, Beauty, Victory all increase in the Cosmos — in fact it is through self development of individual men and women that such Qualities can increase. To desire unity with the universe would be to turn your back on being part of such Work. It may be fine for the weak, but not for us: the adventure is too strong, the goals too worthy.

The ultimate goal of one who Sees the model of Xeper, is not to spit "Xeper" back into the world, but to create a World, by their words and deeds. Yet the enactment of this model, can not but help to cast Xeper into the Objective Universe.

In the religions of *hoi polloi*, the great Good is spreading the religion. These are religions of Foundation (Nomos). They want to teach three things: 1. This is what the Cosmos looks like (you are here). 2. This is where every good person is supposed to go (you can be there). 3. There are laws for the psyche that are as fixed as those in the observable universe.

If that "Good News" were true, it **would** be the moral and ethical imperative of every thinking being to spread the message.

However we know that this is not the case, We know that the
psyche is not bound by Laws exterior to it. (Or as most Setians would say, "What Works for me, may not Work for you."). This simple Truth, places us in opposition to the mechanistic laws of the universe, we are ANTI-nomian. We Teach this: 1. For the secret and the few, there is way of escaping some of the laws of the Cosmos. 2. The Greater freedom you obtain from the Cosmos, the more likely that you will determine your afterlife. (My afterlife will NOT be your afterlife). 3. That the properties of the psyche are acquired by a Willed process, Xeper, the Becoming of Being.

Our imperative is to speak to the secret and the few about who we are. Why is this? Because in their choices they clarify our own.

We see the failures and success of others, Working with the same Knowledge that we (when we are our best) possess. Some remain in the Temple as brief a time as a decade and can point to the World they have made. Needless to say the majority of the World is and must be outside of something as small as the Temple. Others may cling to their Temple-reality because they have done naught in the world. They did not use the Word of Worlds, Xeper is not theirs; although they will have served Set's Eternal Purpose by keeping the Word alive.

The Setian path is as follows:

At first SEPARATION— This is the process of freeing oneself from what one has been told. Most people can not do this. In the worst cases this is manifest by elaborate cosmologies created by new members that "reconcile" Setianism with previously-held cockamamie cosmologies. When you are the most SEPARATE from the Cosmos, you change the fastest. This is the great Secret that Michael Aquino brought to us. It is a profoundly antinomian message in the age of "Oneness with all things." It is — if properly Taught and Understood by the Priesthood of Set the key to our power. It is at the heart of the truly antinomian character of Setian universe — the use of a subjective approach to the subjective universe, which ultimately is the key to Dominion.

Secondly, SYNTHESIS— This puts together an interior world picture. This is very hard to do. Most people would rather pick up someone's existing picture, that of LaVey, or Crowley, Spare, Blavatsky or Webb, etc. The picture empowers them by giving direction to their actions. It both determines lines of inquiry and world building. That is to say it makes you think hard about somethings, and become stronger in that Virtue — and it helps you pick what you want to do today — vacation? Start a business? Take/Teach a class? Paint a painting?

Thirdly REINTEGRATION. This is very hard to do. If we remain a creature of dreams, we may be happy and lucky, but we do not achieve the self-deification that is the Sign of the Word of Worlds. We have to go into the world and make it. We must fashion our kingdoms. In this process many will follow, but a few will come to us and say, "What was your secret? How did you manage to have a happy, powerful life?" To them we give the Secret, for our own education and enjoyment. We Create for ourselves fit companions by the revealing the model of Xeper, just as the Prince of Darkness creates such companions for Himself.

This is not a one-time process. This process goes round and round and round — but each time the effects are greater. Each SEPARATION takes further into field of strong self-knowledge, self commitment, and healthy self-love. Each SYNTHESIS shows more how the Cosmos works, and how we can Work if we Create ourselves according to our self-discovered plan. Each REINTEGRATION brings quantifiably increasing amounts of Pleasure, Wisdom, and Power.

With each turn of the Spiral Force, we bring more people to the Temple. With each turn we further a common Understanding of Xeper, which must always lag far behind our individual understanding. With each turn we create worlds within and beyond us. And on a Cosmic scale with each turn we increase the sum total of possibilities and potentialities in the Cosmos.

Concerning LBM: One of the reasons to practice LBM is the Need to Create a loosening in the warp and weft of the world, so that your Will comes to have more and more of an effect on what is already conditioned and created. This sort of loosening is needed for and Creates four effects. They are:

Freedom Without: The ruling paradigm of the world is (and must be) one of stability. We are in an unspoken social contract with everyone we meet — "I'm not going to change, you're not going to change." Setians, as by-product of their Xeper, are undergoing constant change — particularly in their early stages of their Initiation. So people are often bewildered, angry or distrustful of them. In the world, social control is maintained by spending most of our time talking about the trivia of life in great detail. We tell each other where we eat, how our car is running and so forth. Slowly we each build up a picture of one another in our minds, and base all of our actions and expectations on that picture. If you allow your friends/co-workers/family to know everything about you, they will have a handle on how to make you act, bad feelings when you show freedom — and WORST of all they will continually reinforce their image of you back upon you. People tend to be "enablers." They are not only willing to support you in your alcoholism or drug-abuse — they will support you in anything that furthers their picture of you. So Setians must do three things. One, they must project a slightly mysterious image, so that as change processes occur there are no bad feelings against them. Secondly the Setian must project an idealized image of what he wishes to Become, so that social forces reinforce that idea. If you tell people that you are a scholar, they will praise you/help you with scholarly things. This is a matter of managing external realities to obtain internal ones. Thirdly Setians must avoid letting others know too much about weaknesses that they are trying to overcome. It's all right if they talk to their therapist about this, but not to the guy in the next cubicle at work. Because the other will aid you toward bad behavior as much as good. In essence others must be led to think of you: "I don't have too good a handle on Joe, he's complex and full of nice surprises, but I do know he works really hard to better himself."

Freedom Within: This is the flip-side of the above. One of the ways people create themselves is by constantly telling lies about themselves. You have seen and heard it around you — it can be the successful woman that goes around talking about incompetent she is, or the least-attractive of all men that goes on about being Don Juan. Suddenly it hits you, they *really* believe it. But the depth of this revelation seldom hits you — you have just seen one of the most easily manipulated aspects of Self Creation— yea that Holy thing we call GBM. You too can use it, simply by making list of your faults — let's say your bad at keeping your word — then telling people "I am good at keeping my word." Hearing yourself say things in your voice, will effect your Becoming on a deep level. If you can combine this with the effect above, you are on your way to making yourself and your world.

Protection from Revelation: I learned this years ago from a friend that ran a swinger's club. Now even in the fairly liberal environs of Austin this is a questionable occupation, and not the best way to introduce yourself (to say your dentist or Realtor not to mention your daytime boss). However one of the first things that my friend would tell anyone, was that she had orgies at her house. She would always tell it in a joking tone. For example, "I am busy this weekend, because of that orgy I have every month." Now the joking manner, made most people assume that she was kidding. However over the years, people would find out (and either be amused or hostile), but in the later case she always pointed out that she had told them from the beginning.

Telling the Truth as though it were a joke, can keep the Truth from biting you later. I always tell my friends before I go off to Conclave that I am going to a meeting of the International Satanic Conspiracy and can "say no more" wink, wink. Now they figure I'm off doing some smutty or slightly illegal thing, but when I finally went public about my Temple affiliation, no one was able to accuse me of lying to them, or hiding anything.

Creation of the Network: This is the magical culmination of the first three effects. If you change your fellow beings into believing that you are interesting and skilled in some area, that you are working to become skilled in, they will act as your eyes and ears. If you tell them you are a scholar, they will introduce you to their cousin, who happens to be the best scholar in the field you're interested in. If you tell yourself that you are reliable and daring — you will be able to follow up on leads that people are quite happy to give you. (They see themselves as not daring enough to do so). If you have lead them to believe that you are in some way connected with some Occult secret too dire to talk about, they will come to see you as a powerful person, and desire to connect you with other powerful people in their life. (They will want to show you of to the other people they respect\fear\desire.) In short, the external reality you have crafted will come (in the most unexpected of ways) to have the people you would have dreamed of knowing in it.

This later effect is only of use if, while you have created this illusion of being what you Wish to Be, you have done hard work in actually Becoming it. Then when you have that chance meeting with the film director, occult scholar, gallery owner that your carefully planted LBM seeds has brought, you will have something Real to show the world at the right time. If you don't develop the reality to match the lies, you'll merely be laughed at. Of course to do long term LBM like this, you must have profound knowledge of who you really are, what you really Wish to Become, and a sense of how to get there from here.

In this regard I will leave you with a magical slogan of Austin Osman Spare, "What is a lie, but a mistimed event?"

Note Thirteen

Concerning the Purpose of the Temple: The Purpose of the Temple is to give permission from the Self to the Self to seek after its own Becoming.

Let me give you a very mundane example:

Let's say that you have been trying for some years to quit smoking. The methods have been varied form cold turkey to the patch to gum to acupuncture from a guy in a trailer park named Rollo, Master of the Mystic East. But to no avail.

You come across an old acquaintance that used to smoke like a chimney. He mentions that one day, he just quit.

Suddenly although nothing has apparently changed in your chemistry, you toss the pack of cigarettes away, and you never smoke again.

A common enough story.

But look at its elements. One, a person needing to change, who has been a sincere seeker. Two, a person that has effected the desired change, and Three a Hidden synthesis of the two that effect behavior.

The Temple exists to Create such moments. For some seekers this occurs upon reading the *Crystal Tablet* especially the "Subjective Approach to the Subjective Universe" part of *Black Magic*. For others it happens during a ritual, or at Conclave, or even exchanging a word on one of the lists. The Self remembers the force that Creates it — it briefly Remembers itself and then realizes that that force may be invoked anywhere, at anytime — that the force of Self-creation is not bound to the laws of the mechanistic universe.

Such awakenings can not be planned. We can't put on the calendar, "Wake up on Tuesday." But once Awakened the Self can begin to learn how to create the type of place and circumstances that future Awakenings can occur.

Concerning the Priesthood of Set: The III° is the "merging of the consciousness, indeed the personality, with that of the Prince of Darkness himself." How does such a statement make sense in a LHP environment?

The Left Hand Path is the path of Individuation rather than union. The follower of the *Via sinister* seeks to exalt his or her independence and power.

What are we then to make of the paradoxical state of Being that the Priests of Set claim for themselves?

Let us consider what we can say about the God of Isolate Intelligence.

Firstly he is not the same thing as "intelligence" He struggles with the same fight that his Children do. Indeed Gifting others with consciousness was the method by which He remains separate.

If the universe were full of mechanical beings and only one magician of great power, the universe would simply become the body of that magician in enough time.

The presence of the Gift in Flesh is Necessary, it isn't something Set does on a whim.

Now let us consider the nature of man.

In those rare moments of Xeper, every human being has a profound sense of his or her possibilities. They see how each step they have taken has led to where they are, and the vast unfilled Future spreads out before them. Here by thought and action they can move further from the life laid out for them by society and Nature, and toward a unique state of existence.

Alright that's simple enough. Set needs Free people to introduce and further the possibilities of Individuation, and we effected by that Working seek such moments.

Here we have two sorts of personality, both seeking the same goal of Cosmic freedom. We have Set, a general in the dark army, and we have those daring enough to fight on his side, the privates. (If it helps picture Set as George C. Scott, "Alright you worthless S.O.Bs I want you to hit the beach tomorrow and Xeper!")

Now let us consider the Priest or Priestess.

He or she has the same "marching orders" as anyone else on the Left Hand Path — but the scope of his or her actions is different. Not only must they use the world of matter to make an honest buck, they come to have the Need to use the world of spirit to make more Setians. They encourage others to find what Works for them. They give the same orders, on an individual basis that Set gives on a Cosmic basis. Their consciousness, personality, and concerns are not those of a private now, they have begun to resemble the general. Their development has made them Set-like.

But this is not a merely a case of linear development. Because as they restructure their personalities to become Set-like they have the ability to sense and feel the great Working Set is performing on the Cosmos. They become participants in something larger than themselves, but without submitting to, or being subsumed in it. Their own genius and quest for freedom causes them to demonstrate the Cosmic Working by actions of their own choice.

This interaction with the principle of Isolate Intelligence does not make you part of that principle, but increases that principle within you as you increase it in the world. By this and other methods Set's goal of exporting Xeper to the Objective Universe is obtained.

> Do What Thou Wilt Shall Be The Whole Of The Law. Great Is The Might Of Set, Greater Still He Through Us.

Concerning the Will: Will does not come from the processes of the Cosmos, but from hard actions of individuals. It can be gained and trained.

The Will is an non-mechanistic attractor that works on consciousness, and therefore on events. If invoked without lust for results, It is the single most powerful force that an individual can possess.

The Will brings thought back to Itself. Our thoughts wander everywhere. Within a minute you can think about sex, magic, money, snack foods, your neighbors, elephants, politics and name of that guy in your third grade class that ate paper. The Will, like a magnet keeps bringing thought back to a theme.

The Will can affect the thoughts of others. People will show up in your life, and tell you things. People will give you things. You will have opportunities and strange "failures" that lead to success, if your Will is strong.

The Will is not connected to the mechanistic universe. It isn't what you use to get a new car, or a certain job. It is what you use for general principles, such as Will-To-Wealth. That may help you get a job, or it may help read a certain issue of the *Wall Street Journal* or it may make that banker in the bus listen to your problems.

But more than that It makes you pay attention to what you hear, or have the courage to step into an new area of your life. Once the Will is strong, fear and anxiety begin to disappear.

The Will is made strong by disconnecting it from results.

If you invoke the Will (for say) wealth, you work on keeping the invocation strong. You don't let it get to you that you are still working as a waiter. You look for other work, just like everyone else, but you keep your invocation strong. Eventually — and you will always be surpassed how this snuck up on you — you will have obtained your goal.

If you try to focus your Will on a particular event, you will know failure and sadness and give up the magical Quest.

The Will is not an arrow, shot at a target. It is way of Being that soaks through you into all of your thoughts, words, and deeds — and then out into the world finding either lesser Wills to dominate, or similar of equal Wills to act in synergy with.

From such synergies come the possibilities of Schools of Initiation.

Concerning Objectivity: The Temple of Set has taken Subjectivity as its matrix. In other words, achievement and evolution are guarded by a self-defined form. We don't grade you on how much money you make, what car you drive, or what academic degrees you have. But this does NOT mean that we don't have Objectivity as a cultural value. We have a very clear cultural value. Whatever your desires are, if you are pursuing the Path of Xeper, rather then that of delusion, you will be able see steady movement toward those goals in the objective universe as well as the subjective one. If you're goal is to be a better musician, you will not only work hard to produce music that is better by your own (hopefully high) standards you will also be able to point to better gigs, better recording contracts, the ability to work where and with whom you choose. A matrix of Subjectivity can include — and indeed as long you wish to fight delusion must include — Objectivity. A matrix of Objectivity can not include Subjectivity. So we choose the bigger field, knowing that this does open us to the very real dangers of laziness and wishful thinking. It is every Setian's Self-duty to remain alert and armed against these foes.

If you are undergoing Xeper, the size of what you can cause to happen in the world, must be continually increasing. And this facility being exercised will bring you more opportunities for Xeper than simple human advancement would. The last sentence was a great secret of Greater Black Magic. Read it again.

Concerning Lesser Black Magic: The most useful field to practice Lesser Black Magic is to cause those who could hinder you to momentarily become more powerful by receiving an image of themselves form you. This is minor god-making, and is an Art related to the greater Setian Art of Self-Deification.

On the Left Hand Path we are aware of the human's unnatural need to be more than he or she is. We exalt that Need, it is the Black Flame, which burns to the glory of Desire. We also know that 99.9 per cent of all humans can not exalt that Need, and therefore they suffer — all the time. So most of the time, they turn mean and petty. If you can make them feel they are important or powerful, they will do anything for you, because you have assuaged the pain that actually keeps the Worlds of Horrors going.

Take for example a minor bureaucrat. He is hateful to every poor sap that is caught in his office. But you come to see him and you say, "I really need some help in getting this paperwork done and I know that you're the one that can help me. You're the one that really gets things done around here." You have told him he has power, and he will do anything he can to prove you right.

Or you deal with the department secretary that has turned her ache of inadequacy into a fine mass of passive aggressions. You come to her and say, "I hope you can help me. You know who to ask, what to do. I hope you can teach me." You have told her that she is wise, and she will do anything she can to prove you right.

Lastly the human aching need for recognition has made everyone believe that no one listens to them. If you listen and remember what people say to you, you will command them. Simply saying, "I was struck last Tuesday when you talked about the city's traffic problems." is a great charm.

Learning what needs cause LBM to work, is also learning self-knowledge about what it is to be human. It will teach what you must have, show you how you have been tricked and explain the pageant of human history to you in ways that books never can.

Thusly LBM becomes a guide to the inhabitant of Sol III, and will Teach you not only where you are starting from, but where you stand **all** the time, no matter how great your Xeper. It is a guide that every one can pursue, and its brings Power as well as Knowledge, which marks it firmly as a technique of the Left Hand Path.

Note Fourteen

Concerning Hawaii: The Nineteenth International Conclave began on October 13, XXXIII, the DCXCI anniversary of the arrest of Jacques De Molay and 123 other Knights, proof that his formula of gathering the few to change the world still Works despite the seven hundred years of efforts of pope and king. The elemental forces of water and lava were variously invoked and experienced from the Order of Leviathan's Working in the Ocean to Arkte's rite of the Ocean Mother. The forces of Dream and Imagination were likewise plumbed — both ritually in the Order of the Trapezoid's Work and rationally in the presentations of the Order of the Wells of Weird. On the night that marked the anniversary of Set Slaying Osiris, all of these elements were worked into the main Conclave Working, the Ring of Fire Working. Great strides toward incorporating the use of emotional friction were made in seminars.

Concerning Art: The Magus Gurdjieff claimed that certain art was "Objective" that is to say that it had the same influence on trained and untrained minds, that is to say Art that could cause an increase in Being when viewed, heard, or otherwise experienced.

Such things do not exist. One can not produce a work of art that will lead to a Door opening in all who view it. All that an artist can do is produce a work of art that can express his or her state during production. In this sense great art is like telepathy.

The cultural constraints and context serve to open the Doors for some, and lock them closed for others. One of the most initiatory experiences in my life was reading James Joyce's *Ulysses*. That book opened me to the idea of there being many, many different ways of looking at the world going on at once— and that Being meant Seeing into as many of these as desired. I even understood the postmortem state I desire while reading the book. I want to be the artist — in the scheme of *Ulysses* I want to be the Force that sends Molly, Stephen and Bloom the dream about the melon — and then watches the results.

But for others *Ulysses* brings to mind the remark that Nora addressed to her husband, "James, why can't you write any books that people can read?"

The Egyptian verb "S'Xeper" meaning "it causes one to Xeper" can be applied to art. Most interestingly it can be applied both to art that the artist makes him or herself or art that is merely consumed. The later might seem odd on first thought – after all if Xeper is Self-driven aren't outside sources irrelevant?

But when one comes to understand that "perception is a willed act" then you can grasp that merely opening up to certain images and words can release Being. This happens a good deal at the beginning of one's Quest, and it helps you continue the Quest for more Being.

However these inspiring states are only the smallest step up the ladder of what you may Become.

I leave it as an exercise for all of you to look at people experiencing this Opening. You, your friends, your co-workers . . . maybe you see them "light up" after visiting a gallery, or they have seen that film which they feel everyone should see. Or perhaps they have been Touched by Mozart's Requiem. They are experiencing not the Art — after all other people sat in the same movie theater — but their own unfolding of Being. That feeling is a feeling of Xeper being observed.

What they lack is the understanding that such moments don't belong to the stimulus of art, but to the stimulus of themselves. They don't know that they can learn to make such states in themselves, and that Learning to do so, is the second step toward freeing one's self from the world.

Concerning Lesser Black Magic: As the second High Priest taught, one of the great Secrets of Lesser Black Magic is giving people permission to let their own magic work. The formula is really simple, a friend comes to me and tells her tale of woe, her boss is a jerk, can you do something? Simply look her in the eye and tell her, "It has already been taken care of." This will work on two levels. Firstly most things do take care of themselves, and when things resolve themselves, you will be given credit. (This is how doctors have maintained superstitious awe in their clients for millennia). Secondly, you have given a part of them permission to Do the magic, which they consciously feel they are incapable of Doing. In this second (and rarer) circumstance, they will then look to you for Knowledge, which you must use your wisdom to dispense.

Both of these situations not only make your friends feel better, they up your status in your friends' eyes; and they Teach you something as well. It prepares the way for you to understand that things do resolve themselves — this very important truth will free a good deal of your psychic energy by replacing worry with Planning. Secondly it will let you begin to understand just how **much** magic there is in the world. Of course mainly it is sleeping — as it should be — but you will think about casting your magical nets over a bigger section of the world than before.

Learning that there is a great deal of magic in the world, can bring you both healthful humility and a growing sense of awe of what the world could be. Making contact with that Dream of the World that Could Be, is one of the places where a certain type of immortality can begin. Tricking others into Doing their own magic is ultimately another place to set waves in motion for your own Remanifestation.

Concerning Working in the World One of the best "magical" Understandings of the Past is the Well of Wyrd, Urdhr's Bourne, where each Saying or Doing from the worlds above falls and is blended with every other saying or doing. Your deeds of yesterday are blended equally with the deeds of your ancestors' ancestors. The Hidden source of your thoughts, dreams and insights come up from the Well — and here's the Secret— magicians can send their Sayings and Doings into the well with Conscious intent. Your Deeds can be Done while being Aware/Awake that you are Doing them to change them all magically, just as you are Doing them to change your own life in a rational linear manner. If that Truth can be held in the mind **while** you act. In a very short time your life will change greatly. First your dreams change, then what you see, then your opportunities, and then the rewards of your actions. Look for that cycle, if it isn't happening, then push up your Doings. This is the Secret of the Second Degree.

The model for conscious Work is not one of reaction. Here is what the world teaches: learn your flaws and your hang-ups and then work to overcome them. All self-work is derived from moving away from something bad, or sinful. Here is what the Temple teaches: imagine what you wish to be, and then check everyday to see if your actions are moving toward the idealized state. Of course you will never get there because the powers of your imagination can outstrip your powers of manifestation. You will also have material to will into your Dreams, and Work for in your magic based on the desired state, which should be refined as you Come Into Being.

Now the question for the Initiate is how to pick that idealized state. Should he simply flip through the dictionary and grab a few good words at random — loyal, thrifty, clean, smart and so forth? That would work if all beings were the same, and the goals of their Becoming could be specified. But all Beings are not the same, and the goal of Xeper is to **increase** the amount of individuation in the Cosmos. No, the Setian picks her idealized self based on **experience** — things that she has done and felt — that feel right to her. We experience moments of truly being ourSelves in the world. Only we can Know them. But by being ever vigilant for them, we can begin to see what we are capable of. We can Work to change the inner aspects of out lives so that we can have such states, and we can Work to change the outer aspects of our lives that we can have such states.

Thus the Setian has an ever-clearer idea of what they wish to Become **and** the means to achieving that state.

This notion can inform us on all of our life decisions, from how much money to make, to what companions to have. Such a process enables us to listen very receptively to criticism. We neither run from it, thinking that we are too good to hear it, nor accept it whole hog, thinking we are unworthy. We accept it as a report on our direction that may very well show that we have further to travel than we thought.

One's notion of oneself begins at an unconscious level, and for most people that never changes. One of the most interesting side effects is that our self-image determines whom we are at ease with. If we have made ourselves into victims of abusive relationships or drunks, we will pick similar troubled people as friends. As we adopt the path to more consciousness the times may come when we throw off these (largely hidden) bad self images, and suddenly find that certain people no longer interest us. Likewise if we allow ourselves to deteriorate, persons of quality become uninteresting to us. A good cure for Left Hand Path hubris is to look around at our friends and say "Although I don't know it, I am as screwed up as they." Likewise a test for one's advancement is seeing the overall level of new people that you welcome into your life. This simple external level-taking will tell you more about your level of being than external celebrations of your transformation such as formal Recognition. (This can also help you not to be a Savior god, and help you slay the White Knight within, but I digress).

In the meantime, be looking for notes from your own future.

Leave Taking

I will be sharing other books with you via this special press. I hope that you are willing to talk and think about what you read here with others. My opinions are not dogma, there are shared with you to open you to the Cosmos.

As long as the Temple opens the Door to Set, the door to your hidden self, and the door to your friends in the Yet-To-Be and your ancestors in the Shaping realm, it will flourish. The Working that created it, a joint Working between man and the Shaper of his consciousness, is eternal. The current moment which became visible in 1966, allows you a moment to participate in a more awake fashion. Currently it is very small compared the billions of mankind. Like a single drop running down a green vine deep in Africa, it will become the Nile.

Put the book aside for a moment. Close your eyes. Breathe in. In that quiet of your subjective universe you can feel it. It is up to you if you want to further it.

Great Is The Might Of Set, Greater Still He Through Us.

XEPER
Setnakt
21/6/XXXIX

www.ingramcontent.com/pod-product-compliance
Ingram Content Group UK Ltd.
Pitfield, Milton Keynes, MK11 3LW, UK
UKHW041426180426
11947UKWH00007B/315